*crystal healing
essentials

D0865999

crystal healing
essentials

cassandra eason

foulsham
LONDON • NEW YORK • TORONTO • SYDNEY

foulsham

The Publishing House, Bennetts Close, Cippenham, Slough,
Berkshire, SL1 5AP, England

ISBN 0-572-02735-4

Printed in Great Britain by Cox & Wyman Ltd, Reading, Berkshire.

Contents

Introduction

The power of crystals

Hold a crystal, any crystal, large or small, or a crystal sphere. Gaze into its depths, then close your eyes, letting your psychic senses come to the fore. In your mind, with your inner psychic, clairvoyant eye, you may see single images, scenes or other worlds. With your clairaudient, psychic ear you may hear sounds of the sea, the rainforest or a city street, music, song or poetry. As you run your fingers across the surface you may feel, through psychometric or psychic touch, heat, cold, or a sense of peace or joy. People using crystals for the first time have experienced all of these sensations, through the same channels by which healing energies are given and received.

You may, however, sense nothing as you hold the crystal, and this is normal too. For some people, it takes some time, perhaps a few days or even weeks of working with crystals, to regain the natural instinctive connection we all have with crystalline energies.

Crystal healing in history

The power of crystals is timeless, ageless. They were regarded as living sentient essences in societies where traditional ways were unbroken until comparatively recently. Their powers amplify the innate self-healing powers of humans and enhance our natural ability to heal loved ones, animals and even places.

The Native North Americans call this link the sacred hoop or circle of existence, whereby positive energies can be passed from one species to another.

We have no real idea when crystal healing began. But we can be fairly sure that the crystals used by early humankind would not have resembled the highly polished stones we have today, shipped from far-flung parts of the world and tumbled to remove every imperfection. Instead, theirs were crystals that could just be discerned, glinting through grey or brown rock, found on shores, hillsides or riverbanks close to their settlements.

Such crystals were part of the earliest magic, as depicted in palaeolithic cave paintings, which showed hunters wearing animal skins and antlers, dancing to imitate the coming of the herds and the hunting of the animals. Their performances were more than superstitious play-acting: they were attuning their minds to those of the animals, and this had an entirely practical intent. *Where are the herds going next? When I stalk a particular creature how will it react, what will it feel? Will it stand still, run, attack?*

Written records of crystal healing can be found dating from earliest times. One of the most famous healing stones was a diamond reputed to have belonged to Abraham, who is mentioned in Genesis, the first book of the Old Testament. The stone was reputed to cure instantly any sick person who looked on it, and when Abraham died, it was re-absorbed by the Sun.

The Papyrus Ebers, dating from about 2500 BC, lists the healing properties of particular gems, including lapis lazuli for eye salves, haematite for stopping and preventing haemorrhages, emeralds to cure dysentery and rubies for liver and spleen diseases.

Plato, the Greek philosopher who lived from 427 to 347 BC, claimed that stars and planets converted decayed and decaying material into the most perfect gemstones and that these stones then came under the rule of those planets and stars. Engraving crystals was therefore believed to have greater power when the Sun was in a certain constellation or when the moon or one or more of the planets was in ascendant at the time. What is more certain is that stones such as topaz and moonstone become more powerful as the Moon waxes, achieving maximum strength for healing on the full Moon.

The Greek pharmacist Dioscorides described in his *Materia Medica* over 200 crystals and gems that could be used for healing, and the *Natural History* of Pliny, the first-century Roman chronicler, provides another source of crystal healing knowledge. In it, he preserves the older teachings and repeats their important theory that the cure of different diseases depended on both the colour and the substance of the stone.

However, crystal healing would seem to operate on a spiritual and magical rather than a physical, or medical, level – though the ancients would argue these are inseparable in triggering the body and mind's immune system. It is true that both the Ancient Egyptians and the Chinese, and indeed alchemists until the eighteenth century, did crush gems and add them to medicines, but the therapeutic power of stones acts primarily on a less tangible level. During the Middle Ages, healing gems were placed on the shrines of saints and were accorded religious as well as magical powers. One example is the sapphire on the shrine of St Erkinwald in Old St Paul's Cathedral in London. This was donated in 1391 by Richard Preston, a London grocer, who made the offering so that people visiting the shrine might be cured of eye diseases.

Using the power of crystals

We do not know how the power of crystals actually works, but, to put things in a modern context, it would seem likely that crystals act as transmitters, passing not only their own energies, but those of the Earth and cosmos to a sick or distressed person, animal or place.

It is this same power that makes children so psychic. When children act out encounters with dragons or princesses, they are not pretending in the way that adults do; they actually merge with the characters they have created. Children have the same affinity for connecting with the powers of crystals. Give a child a bag of crystals and, if asked, he or she will automatically select, for example, an amethyst to soothe a migraine or an orange-banded agate for a stomach pain. It this open, instinctive attitude of mind that makes for a successful crystal healer.

At the end of this chapter I have suggested a visualisation, a process through which you can practise merging with a crystal, and enable its powers to blend via telepathic waves with your own psychic abilities. In this way you will be able to transfer its energies to heal both yourself and others.

The power emanating from crystals is more than mere speculation. The Russian scientist Semyon Kirlian discovered that both inorganic and organic gems are surrounded by a radiating energy field that can be captured by special photographic techniques. Each has its own specific appearance and therefore its own individual properties. Rose quartz, amethyst and clear crystal quartz seem naturally tuned for healing work, and these three crystals can be used for virtually all forms of healing.

Gems and crystals have been used in many ways: crushed into powders or pounded into ointments, soaked in water that was then drunk by the sufferer, even simply placed on painful areas of the body or carried as amulets.

Engraving on gems and crystals the image of a god or a symbol of natural power was believed to increase the power of these stones, and it is this talismanic or symbolic healing function that has become most important in modern crystal healing. Though placing crystals in water and drinking the liquid is part of crystal healing – as is breathing in crystalline light – the effect is regarded as a spiritual rather than a physical transference of energies. This makes crystals a potent method for absent healing, as the energies flow from one soul to another.

Crystals in folk magic

Over the centuries, crystals have been incorporated into folk magic and healing work, combining both symbolic and practical application. For example, in Scandinavia, Denmark, Germany, the UK and lands in which the Anglo-Saxon influence was strong, clear quartz crystal spindle whorls were used in spinning; when turned the spindle would catch the light and suffuse the thread with rainbows. Garments were infused with protective or empowering charms by the chanting of spells and incantations as they were sewn. Such magical spinning and weaving processes remained popular until mediaeval times throughout northern Europe. They were used especially to create garments to be worn by soldiers and explorers to keep them safe from harm and to ensure that any wounds would quickly heal. Chanting or talking still forms an important part of crystal therapeutic work.

This spinning magic would have been amplified by the specific powers of the crystal from which the spindles were fashioned. Clear crystal quartz would be a favourite choice, since it was a source of the life force itself, bringing health, energy and clarity of purpose. In addition, it would be used to channel the power of sunlight and moonlight; so, for important ventures, thread would be spun first in bright sunlight and then on the full Moon. Spindle whorls were also made of amber and jet. Amber was called the tears of Freyja, the Viking goddess of love, beauty and fertility, and so endowed the wearer of the magical garment with courage and confidence, radiance and sexual magnetism. Jet, used for adornments and amulets since the Bronze Age, was fiercely protective, especially for sailors and those who crossed the seas for trade or conquest.

Crystal healing for everyone

Many crystals are true precious stones, and these have always had a fascination for the rich and wealthy. Over the centuries, the perfection of individual stones and their rarity were believed to increase their healing potency. Indeed, crystal healing, in spite of the demise of other forms of ancient medicine, retained its popularity, although, as I have said, the emphasis did change from physical to spiritual applications. This may have been because gem healing remained the province of those who could afford such stones and so they were relatively impervious to persecution and scorn. The Russian Tsar, Ivan the Terrible, who died in 1584, displayed his collection of healing gems to Sir Jerome Horsey, the envoy of Queen Elizabeth I of England. He told the envoy:

Diamond restrains furie and luxurie; the ruby is most comfortable to the heart, brain, vigar and memorie of man, clarifies congealed and corrupt blood. In sapphire I greatle delight; yt preserves and increaseth courage, joins the heart, is pleasing to all the vital senses, precious and verie sovereigne for the eye, clears the sight, takes away bloodshott and strengthens the mussels and the stringes.

However, even ordinary families might have a special gem or crystal, brought back by a sailor relation from the Orient or some tropical island, and this would be handed down through the generations. It would be brought out when a family member or even a neighbour was sick, and so such stones acquired healing reputations. In my family we were relatively poor, but I remember, as a child, being shown a family opal ring. Opals are sometimes considered unlucky, but this stone became an amulet against all manner of sickness. I have no idea what happened to it after my mother died and I left home, but it was very precious in childhood and always heralded a recovery to health when it was brought out.

Among ordinary people the symbolism of colour was particularly significant, following the universal magical principle of like attracts like or, in its more elevated form, *similia similibus curantur.* This played a very important part in recommending particular stones for specific diseases, and it is interesting to note that these are frequently the same in cultures from entirely separate parts of the world. In Europe, red or red-flecked stones, whether a precious ruby or the humbler green bloodstone (said to have acquired its red markings when the blood of Christ fell on green jasper at the crucifixion), were believed to bring calm and soothe inflammatory conditions as well as relieving diseases of the blood or blood pressure. In much the same way, heart-shaped bloodstones were used by South American Indians. They were dipped in water and held by a patient in his or her right hand to stop bleeding.

Another traditional belief was that healing gems should be worn on different parts of the body that acted as channels to various areas of the body, brain and spirit. For example, the jacinth would be worn around the neck or on the index finger, the diamond on the left arm, the sapphire on the ring finger, the emerald on the index finger and the ruby or turquoise on either the index or the little finger

The ancient traditions of crystal healing and magic have remained constant throughout history. Viking women collected amber and rock crystal from the beaches for their domestic healing magic, and this continued as part of the folk wisdom in Iceland until comparatively recently, despite the fact Christian law forbade the use of 'curing stones' and crystal amulets. When I was in Sweden last spring, I went with some Swedish healers to the shore where they still gather quartz and amber just as their ancestors did more than a thousand years earlier.

Many of the modern healing associations with specific crystals are remarkably consistent through different ages, whether the crystal lore is derived from the Orient or Native North America. For example, the Celts boiled clear crystal quartz and drank the crystal water over nine days to increase their energy levels and cleanse their system. Clear quartz water is still added to baths and splashed on pulse points to restore flagging spirits or relieve exhaustion. Blue lace agate water and water made from other pale blue crystals was used by the Ancient Greeks to relieve a sore throat and also to help a speaker to express words that came from the heart. Today many New Age lecturers and broadcasters, myself included, drink water in which the crystal has been soaked to stop dry throats and coughs while talking.

Crystal healing in the modern world

Although the traditions remain constant, new crystals are still being discovered that have powers commensurate with the needs of our modern-day society. For example, the rich purple and pink sugilite or the more delicate pink and violet kunzite are remarkably protective against noise, technological pollution, the jangling of mobile phones and faxes and the constant frantic pace of today's non-stop urban world. However, the appearance of these crystals is not as unexpected as it may first seem. According to the Gaia Hypothesis (an ecological concept named after the Ancient Greek Earth Mother and first proposed by James Lovelock, a British biologist, and Lynne Margulis, a microbiologist, in the early 1970s), the Earth is a biological self-regulating mechanism. It is therefore not surprising that new crystals have sprung forth in response to modern-day ills. This idea of a sentient Earth Mother is actually one that dates back to the beginning of human consciousness. It continued among indigenous peoples such as the Native North Americans and Australian Aborigines long after the Age of Reason and industrialisation encouraged urban humankind to regard the Earth as a larder and fuel store that could be raided and need never be replenished or kept clean.

Traditional crystals too have found new uses in our technological age. Black tourmaline and malachite are believed to reduce domestic radiation, especially from microwaves and stereos; some people also keep malachite near computers and in workplaces for the same reason.

Crystal healing and you

We all have innate healing powers. Every time a mother rubs a child's hurt knee or a person places a hand on a partner's aching brow, healing energies are transmitted via the love between the people. This means that you can, even with no previous experience, use crystals to heal yourself, your friends and family, and it is for this reason that so many healers first discover their gift through healing a close relative.

Empathy is important for successful healing and that is why the in-built talking time of any session, particularly with strangers, is so crucial. Absent healing also works best if you know the person or have a love of the animal or place on which you are focusing your energies. Sometimes the most spiritually elevated people are not the best healers because they are unable to channel their abilities through a love of individuals rather than abstract humanity.

Methods of crystal healing

If you want to work professionally as a healer, I would recommend that you take formal training through one of the healing organisations listed in the back of the book (see pages 184–7). This book is intended to offer a basic introduction to different methods of using your healing crystals for both direct (or contact) healing and for absent healing work. I explain how different crystals are effective for particular illnesses and disharmony; how you can use them to cleanse and empower your aura, or psychic energy field; and how to unblock and energise these energy channels and the psychic power points or chakras through which energy enters and leaves both our physical and inner-spirit, or etheric, body.

After you have read the first three chapters, which give you a necessary introduction to the properties and uses of crystals, you can read the chapters of the book in any order, and if any part seems irrelevant to you and your life, then you can leave it out entirely. For example, you do not have to understand all about chakras and the aura in order to heal with crystals, though the concepts are valuable in understanding the human energy system.

Once you have learned about basic protection and read some suggestions for beginning healing work, you can just follow your instinctive wisdom; it is quite possible to be a gifted healer without any formal training. However, I hope that by reading through all the sections, you may find ways of enhancing your innate powers and of directing these natural powers in the most effective ways. At the end of the book I have listed further reading that will help you to extend your knowledge if you wish.

Whether you use one particular healing crystal or many, crystal healing will improve your personal well-being and harmony as well as that of those you heal. As you work, your own psychic and spiritual powers will also spontaneously evolve and you will find that your powers of clairvoyance and psychometry emerge in other areas of your life and help you to make wise decisions.

You may find that just one particular method of healing works well for you or that you combine a number of the techniques I suggest throughout the book. However you work, before long you will have developed a unique relationship with your crystals and will heal not only people but also animals and places. As you work, your healing energies will blend with those in the natural world as well as with those of other healers in different places. The release of this creative light into the cosmos will, as a bonus, help to restore the balance of the ecosystem that humankind has neglected and despoiled.

Merging with your crystal

This process demonstrates everything I have said about using crystals. It is not a ritual or ceremony that has to be exactly right, and there is not even any need to worry about how to choose the correct crystal. Simply relax and select any large crystal or crystal sphere to which you feel naturally drawn; allow the same instincts to guide your thoughts.

Wait until after dusk and surround your crystal with a horseshoe of purple candles. Burn sandalwood, frankincense or myrrh incense sticks or cones to enhance your psychic awareness.

* Gaze into the crystal and very slowly breathe in the coloured light through your nose and gently exhale any darkness or greyness though your mouth.

* Continuing to breathe in the crystalline light, draw it around you and visualise yourself within a huge crystal through which the purple candlelight filters.
* Imagine your boundaries dissolving so that the crystalline radiance can flow freely within as well as around you.
* Hear the crystal breathing and feel the gentle vibration it makes as though it was your own heartbeat.
* Allow images to form of the deep volcanic fires, the rushing waters, the cool breezes and the rich soil that caused its formation and of the land from which the crystal came.
* Now let the images fade and, continuing to breathe gently and regularly, be filled with the light and the sound of your images. Sense the way that the crystal is rooted in the Earth, the sky, fire and water.
* Feel its energies melting any rigidity remaining within you and filling you with a clear, liquid energy that gently swirls and spirals.
* When you are ready, gently draw your boundaries around you again so that the crystalline light forms a halo around you and then separates so you are holding the crystal and can still feel its energies.

If when you are healing you can recall the sensation of becoming the crystal, then you can instinctively make connection through it with your patient and know where the source of the disease or discomfort resides – this may be different from the site of the pain or distress. You can then allow the spiralling liquid energy to flow through you via the crystal and your fingertips and into the person you are healing or, for your personal healing, circuiting back through you. This liquid crystal will flow into any dark places, clearing stagnation, restoring, regenerating, and you yourself will feel not depleted but healed and energised, even if you are directing the crystal power into another.

If you can make time weekly, even a few minutes, to merge with a crystal, then when you do heal, the process will become quite spontaneous.

Chapter 1
Preparing for Crystal Healing

As I said in the Introduction, you can heal with absolutely any crystal. What is more, appearance is no guide to effectiveness. Some of the most gifted healers work with what may at first appear like a dull brown or black stone but which once they start healing becomes visibly lighter, glows and may even give off sparks.

You may already own crystals, and you can use these for your healing work. However, you may like to buy a special set of healing crystals, collected over a period of months. Later in this chapter, I will give a list of what I consider to be a comprehensive set of healing crystals, but you certainly do not need to buy them all at once and you can manage perfectly well with a smaller, basic set.

You do, however, need two sizes of crystals: some should be small enough to hold in your hand for contact healing and for placing in water to make crystal potions. You also need larger pieces or spheres of polished or unpolished crystal that can act as a focus for healing light and also for meditation and visualisation.

Basic equipment for crystal healing

Your essential requirements for healing are very simple. Just three crystals will fulfil nearly every need.

Crystal quartz

This clear white stone will give fast results and has the advantage that it can be substituted for any other crystal. Specifically, it is the best choice for unblocking stagnant energies and for infusing energy, light and positive feelings into a person who is ill or sad. Clear quartz will trigger the body's immune system and innate regenerative powers. It also helps if a person is exhausted or being drained emotionally. Some people work with a quartz that is pointed at one end to direct energies, but this is a matter of choice

Citrine

This pure sparkling yellow sun crystal is naturally warming and is gentler than crystal quartz. Capable of melting pain and tension, it encourages the gentle flow of warming energies that will create a sense of well-being and re-balance the body. Citrine unfolds its energies gradually. It also dissolves stress caused by money worries.

Rose quartz or amethyst

These pink or purple transparent crystals are soothing, especially for children. They will remove pain or tension, replacing them with calm and the slow infusion of healing energies. Both of these crystals will dissolve stress caused by problems with relationships.

In addition to these three crystals, you will require one larger item: a crystal quartz pendulum. This is one of the most valuable healing, cleansing and empowering tools. Pendulums, particularly small ones, are not at all expensive. Do make sure you choose crystal quartz. (You may already own a pendulum of a different kind, for dowsing for example, but these are not suitable for crystal work.)

You may also wish to buy a clear crystal sphere or ball. You can heal with quite a small sphere and so it need not be expensive, although, like the pendulum, it should be made of crystal rather than glass.

This basic set may be adapted to all your needs. However, there are many more crystals that can be added to your collection as and when you need them. Later in the book I give more lists of crystals for different aspects of healing: in Chapter 7, I list those that are suitable for chakra or psychic energy work and on page 56 I suggest pairs of stones for contact healing. Additionally, in Chapter 11, I give a more comprehensive list of 50 stones and their healing properties.

Choose from any of the lists to find those you would like to add to your basic collection for specific purposes that are relevant to your life – for example, for protection against environmental pollution or personal hostility, or to alleviate a chronic condition.

Healing crystals for your collection

Agates
Colours: Opaque red, orange, yellow, brown, black, banded and single colour

Agates balance bodily energies and bring harmony to the mind and emotions. Red, yellow and orange agates soothe the stomach, colon, liver, spleen and kidneys and help with discrimination of what is of worth. Black agates help block harmful radiation and protect against negativity. Blue lace agate soothes throats and helps communication of true feelings. Green and moss agates are crystals of the environment and also stimulate the immune system.

Amber
Colours: Orange, occasionally brown, semi-transparent

Amber is an organic gem and can be up to 50 million years old. It is said to contain the power of many suns. It is good for fertility and all digestive and stress disorders, protecting against harm, physical, emotional and psychic. Use it for detoxification and protection from over-exposure to computers and other industrial pollutants.

Fluorite
Colours: Transparent stones in rainbow colours

These will heal the whole system. Green, clear white and lavender are all good for work with chakras (see page 110) and will clear blocked or stagnant energies in the body and mind. Lavender will cleanse and protect the workplace and reduce stress and hyperactivity. Fluorites are sufficiently gentle to heal animals.

Kunzite
Colours: Pink, lilac and purple

A potent stone, sometimes known as the woman's stone because of its ability to soothe female disorders. It increases the ability to give and receive love and is good for overcoming compulsive behaviour and addictions. It reduces mood swings and opens psychic and spiritual channels for divination and healing. Keep kunzite in the car for reducing road rage and tensions, and keep it at work for holding stress at bay.

Jade

Colours: Many shades of green

Jade is the gentlest of stones, good for arthritis, rheumatism and kidney and bladder problems, especially water retention. It protects against spite and anger in others and enhances self-love, especially if there has been destructive behaviour by other people. It connects the user with Earth energies and so alleviates anxiety and panic attacks, and it offers protection against injury and accidents. Jade is a powerful crystal for healing the environment.

Smoky quartz

Colours: Grey or brown to black; semi-transparent when held up to the light

Smoky quartz is traditionally associated with removing negative influences on the user, both physical and emotional. It will transform anger or resentment into positive action, speed recovery from chronic or debilitating conditions and break the cycle of destructive emotional patterns. It is also effective for promoting fertility.

Caring for your crystals

Once you have a core set of healing crystals, you should keep them wrapped in white silk when you are not using them. Roll each one separately to avoid scratching and then keep them together in a velvet drawstring bag. Place larger ones in individual drawstring bags. Choose a big bag for keeping and carrying the whole set. There are a number of evening bags or beaded and sequinned ethnic ones that are perfect, or you can make your own.

Your crystals also need to be empowered regularly with the natural forces of light. There are two ways to do this. On the night of the full Moon, place your crystals in the moonlight from moonrise to moon set, if possible out of doors. (Look in a newspaper or your diary to find the time of the month when the Moon is full.) At least once a month, expose them also to sunlight from dawn until noon.

Finally, on the summer solstice (around 21 June, or 21 December in the southern hemisphere), when the sun is at its most powerful, leave them from the previous dusk until noon on the longest day itself.

Do this in addition to the regular cleansing and charging which I describe on pages 35–9.

A healing sanctuary

Once you have your equipment ready, you might like to create a specific place in your home for your healing work and meditations. You may be lucky enough to have a spare room, or perhaps you can just set aside a quiet corner.

Wherever it is, you will need something to serve as an altar. This can be a table or a shelf, or if you have an old cupboard you can cover it with a cloth and use the storage space to keep your equipment in.

On your altar, place a single pure beeswax or white candle as symbol of the unity of all life and the one divine source that flows through deity, humankind, animal, birds, fish, trees, plants and stones.

You could also keep one or two of your larger crystals here, perhaps your crystal sphere and spheres or unpolished pieces of amethyst and rose quartz. Arrange them with some other smaller crystals, keeping them in a dish or circled around your healing candle so that the light shines on them.

Bless these altar crystals before use by passing them three times clockwise over the healing candle flame and reciting a healing mantra, for example:

Heal and bless, empower and protect, illuminate and sanctify.

Alternatively, you can bless them in the name of light and love, or any deity, angel or archangel on whom you focus.

If there is room and enough light, your altar could also hold growing pots of healing herbs: lavender, the all-healer; gentle chamomile, which is especially good for children's ills and for encouraging gentleness of words; basil for increase in all things and to keep away harm; sage, the herb of long life and health; indeed any that are indigenous to your region that you associate with increase and happiness.

Have a dish for seasonal flowers, fruit, nuts and seeds that will be empowered by the healing energies. These can regularly be given to anyone feeling tired or anxious, not forgetting yourself – if you eat them, you are literally as well as symbolically absorbing the healing energies according to one of the oldest magical principles in existence.

Later in the book I will tell you how to create and use empowered salt and Moon and Sun water. Keep these on or near your altar, too. You may also keep bottles of more traditional sacred water that many healers still prefer for healing ills of both the body and the soul (see pages 38–9 for making this).

To the side in a box, or in drawers within the altar if you adapt a cupboard, you can keep all you need for your healing work. This may include healing oils and incenses (see pages 42–8), smudge sticks (see pages 40–1), favourite flower essences and coloured bottles with stoppers, containing empowered crystal water (see pages 81–3).

Finally, you might like to have a special book in which you can keep a record of your crystal healing.

Creating a healing book

Your healing book could contain the names of any people you know who need healing, plus perhaps pets, a hospital or hospice with which you have connections, sanctuaries for injured creatures, and threatened places and species of wildlife. You can also record in a 'loving connections' section the names of friends or family members who are away from home and may be feeling lonely and also of anyone from whom you are estranged. Write each name on a separate sheet, and under it record any special healing rituals carried out on their behalf, any direct healing you gave and any crystals that seemed especially helpful.

When the person recovers or the situation is resolved in any way – even if they move beyond the sphere of your healing – you can place their name in another section of the book so that the healing crystals and candles on the altar continue to shine light and love on them, even though your direct intervention has diminished.

Using your healing book

Of course, you cannot – and should not – try to focus or help every cause every day. It is sufficient to set aside a special healing time – 10 pm is the traditional healing hour – on just one evening of the week.

* First light your healing candle.
* Place one of your large healing crystals in the candlelight so that the crystalline radiance is reflected over the pages of your healing book.
* Read each of the names in turn, pausing at any that seem especially of concern, and send love by visualising the crystalline light flowing to wherever the person, animal or place is, through the candle flame.
* You may, if you have time, decide afterwards to send extra healing light to one of the names.

Sending healing to an individual

You can use a photograph, newspaper cutting or symbol of the person, animal or place to which you are sending healing energies. You can also use an empowered sachet of herbs as a representative (see pages 96–7 for instructions for making these).

Fill a dish with Sun water for an acute condition or where energy is needed, or Moon water for more gentle healing, or sacred water. Note also the use of the magical number nine, the number of completion.

* Hold the symbol between your hands and speak a few words of love and reassurance as though the person were with you or you were at the lake or woodland under threat.

* Circle your crystal pendulum, healing crystal or crystal sphere over the sachet or symbol nine times anti-clockwise, saying as a mantra:

Go pain and sorrow, change to star or sunbeam, transformed in joy and in tranquillity.

* Plunge the crystal or pendulum into the water or, for a sphere, sprinkle water over it and hold it to the light so that the drops of water fall off and scatter as rainbow light beams all around the symbol. (Mirrors are another good way to reflect light beams off your crystals for healing, as are rainbow crystals or the crystal 'suncatchers' that are popular in America, hung at windows or where they will reflect on the altar.)

* Now circle the pendulum nine times clockwise over the symbol again, saying:

Sun, moon or star beam, rays of light, replace, restore, renew, rejoice.

* Blow out the candle, sending the light to the sick or sorrowing person, saying:

Go light of healing, radiance of love, friendship to where you are needed most this night – (name the person, animal or location). *May blessings fall, darkness and doubts recede into nothingness. So may it be in the name of all that is good and loving and pure.*

If you are feeling ill, worried or afraid, you can go to your healing place and light the candle, holding your favourite crystal and expressing softly your needs and fears. However, the more healing you carry out for others, the more harmony will fall on you. This reward follows from the Threefold Law of magic, which says whatever you give with a willing heart and mind will be returned threefold to you.

Empowering your crystal for a specific purpose

Crystal healing automatically directs energies to wherever they are needed in the body, mind or soul. However, you can focus even more accurately on a specific area of the body or a place by naming your intention or purpose as you empower the appropriate crystal. This is particularly useful for absent healing or for healing the environment. So, for example, if you want to bring life back to an area of land that has been despoiled, choose an environmentally associated crystal, such as the green moss agate. Endow it with specific greening powers, focusing all its energies on triggering regeneration (see pages 73–9 for colour crystal meanings).

The size of the crystal is not important, as its energy field, or aura, is not directly related to its physical mass and can be increased by the ritual performed.

The following ritual demonstrates how you would carry out the empowering programme from start to finish, to ensure continuing healing from the crystal on its chosen focus.

A crystal ritual to restore a woodland

You could use a picture of the place as a focus for the ritual, or, as I do here, make a pot of herbs the symbol for it. Basil, sage and lavender are especially good, but you can use any fast-growing herb indigenous to your region. In this way, it is possible to work in your healing sanctuary and to continue the healing over a period of days without the need to travel. After the ritual, however, you might like to visit the actual place to bury one of your empowered crystals and perhaps to plant a sapling or some seeds. Note this time, the use of the magic number three.

* Light a circle of small green candles (green is the colour of gradual growth and of environmental issues) around the pot of herbs.
* To the immediate north of the symbol (the direction of the ancient element Earth) and within the candle circle, set a small dish of empowered salt (see page 38). Salt is the sacred substance associated with Earth.
* Light two or three patchouli incense sticks in a container to the east of the symbol (this is the direction of the ancient element of Air, whose sacred substance is incense). Patchouli is a fragrance that is very potent in all matters of healing the planet.
* To the south of the symbol, still within the green candle circle, light a pale blue candle for healing. (South is the direction of the ancient element of Fire.)
* Finally, burn cleansing pine or cedar oil in the west (the direction of the ancient element Water). Alternatively, use a small dish of sacred water (see pages 38–9).

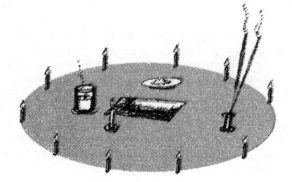

* Take five moss agate stones or five jade crystals. Both of these are especially potent for healing nature and are called the gardeners' crystals. If you cannot obtain them, use any gentle green crystals.
* Place the crystals in a dish and, holding the dish above the salt, sprinkle a few grains of salt over them, saying:

Heal the woodland, restore the trees, the greenery and the living creatures of the forest, Mother Earth.

* Next, take the dish to the incense and, holding one of the sticks, make three clockwise smoke circles around the crystals, saying:

Heal the air, Father Sky, that it may be pure. Let the trees grow tall that they may breathe their life-giving oxygen in a continuing exchange of life power.

* Taking the blue candle in the south, draw a circle of fire around the dish of crystals, saying:

Brother Fire, Summer Sun of the warm South, give light and energy to the new growth, burning away all that is polluted or destructive to rebirth.

* Finally, holding the dish in the west, either pass it three times clockwise over the oil vapour or sprinkle three drops of water over it, saying:

Sister Water, rivers flowing free, fall as gentle nourishing rain that the leaves may be green and the sap rise skywards with the blossoming branches.

* Plant four of the crystals at each of the compass points in the soil around the herbs, saying as a chant:

  Go forth, increase and multiply. Light and love intensify, from the Earth to the Sky.

* Extinguish the oil, but leave around the plant the incense and candles to burn through and the dish with the remaining crystal. You can leave the fifth crystal on your healing altar until you are able to plant it in the woodland.

Chapter 2
Crystals and Protection

Crystals are extremely powerful tools for protection as well as healing. However, both of these actions involve a great deal of energy interchange and so the crystals you use can easily become depleted. Even those you keep in your special healing place and which are constantly absorbing healing light can become filled with the negative energies acquired during healing work. This can not only make them less effective as healing channels but also cause negativity or exhaustion to spill over into your own energy field.

Charging and cleansing your crystals

Cleansing and empowering your crystals is therefore a vital part of your healing work. It will, in addition, provide psychic protection for both the crystals and you. At the end of this chapter I have suggested psychic protection rituals that, especially if you are an inexperienced healer, will help you to remain strong and healthy while helping others. I have also mentioned ways of ensuring that your special healing place is kept spiritually pure.

It is a good idea to cleanse any crystal you have just bought or been given to remove all the vibrations of the people who made, packed and sold it. These are not necessarily negative, but it is important that you create your own personal connections with your healing crystals from the beginning and avoid the impressions of unrelated people diluting the energy flow.

After cleansing, you need to charge your crystal with power so that the innate energies are amplified by the powers of the natural world, the Earth and the cosmos, and the higher powers of goodness and light. You will need to cleanse and recharge your crystals every week and immediately after carrying out an intense healing session either for yourself or someone else. If you do use crystals for personal protection in the workplace, home or therapeutic setting, they will need regular cleansing.

Many of the traditional methods combine cleansing and empowering. I have listed a number that I have found effective.

Quick cleansing

If you are in a hurry or have to work away from home, you can instantly cleanse and empower a crystal by holding it under running water, shaking it dry and holding it up to the light, repeating in your mind a mantra, such as:

Darkness and pain flow away, light and gladness only stay.

Cleansing and empowering crystals using a crystal pendulum

This is the simplest and most effective method of cleansing and empowering.

* Hold a clear crystal pendulum over the stone or a circle of stones that are to be cleansed.
* Pass the pendulum over the crystals nine times in slow anti-clockwise circles, seeing darkness draining out of the crystals into the pendulum with each sweep.

* Plunge your pendulum nine times either into a bowl of sacred water (see pages 38–9) or hold it for a few seconds, nine times in rapid succession under any source of running water. Visualise the darkness flowing away.
* Shake the pendulum in sunlight if possible.
* Move the pendulum slowly nine times clockwise over the stones for empowerment, visualising glowing energies emanating from the pendulum and entering the crystals.
* Keep your pendulum well charged and positive by running it under cold, clear water and then leaving it in water steeped with rose petals over which a cleansing and empowering incense such as pine and a white candle flame have been passed clockwise.

Cleansing and empowering crystals with salt and water

This is one of the oldest methods of purifying and endowing spiritual strength, which can be used not only for crystals but also in many forms of ritual for protection and power. Once you have made supplies of sacred salt and water, you can store them in closed containers and use them to represent the elements of Earth and Water respectively to give a formal crystal healing ceremony more power. You can also use empowered salt and water to imbue herbs with healing power. The herbs can then be placed in sachets and used in crystal ceremonies of absent healing (see Chapter 6).

Making empowered salt

* Place sea salt in a ceramic dish on your healing altar and light a pure beeswax candle at each of the four main compass points around the edges of the altar. (Beeswax was sacred to the Mother Goddess and later the Virgin Mary.)

* Light the four candles, beginning in the north. Say at each quarter of the circle:

I dedicate this salt only to the greatest good and for healing, asking that Divine Light and blessing may enter, purify and empower.

* Leave the candles to burn down. (Make sure they are in broad-based holders so wax does not fall on the salt.)

Making sacred water

You can use either pure spring water or tap water left in a crystal or clear glass container in the open air for a 24-hour cycle beginning at dawn. Some people like to make their sacred water on the night of the full Moon. Since this rises about sunset, you can follow the old Celtic day that began at sunset and continue until the next sunset. Some practitioners, following the ancient Celtic tradition, prefer to boil two litres (about four pints) of water to which nine quartz crystals have been added. Alternatively, you may be able to obtain water from a sacred spring or holy well if there is one in your area, but it is a good idea to empower water for your own use.

The following is an alternative, more complex method, but I find it particularly effective.

* Take a crystal quartz – used in many cultures to energise and purify water. Wash it well to remove any impurities introduced by the modern world and then place it in the bottom of a glass bowl.
* Into the bowl pour mineral water, from a sacred source if possible.
* Leave the bowl in a circle of white flowers or blossoms for 24 hours, where it will absorb the full light cycle.
* Finally pass over it a twig from one of the protective trees – rowan, ash, palm, thorn or olive. Do this first nine times anti-clockwise to remove any lingering negativity, and then nine times clockwise to empower it.
* When the water is empowered, add three pinches of the empowered salt. Using a pendulum or pointed crystal quartz, stir the salt into the water three times clockwise and then make either the conventional sign of the cross or the diagonal cross that represents the power of the Earth Mother, saying:

Salt and water, cross of light, power of healing, enter bright. Shining crystal, gifts unfold, moonlight silver, sunlight gold.

Keep your sacred water in a clear glass bottle with a stopper.

Cleansing and empowering crystals with sacred salt and water

* Make three clockwise circles of salt round your crystals, followed by three circles of sacred water beyond the salt circles.
* Say:

Circles three of salt, cleansing of the Earth, blessings on these crystals, healing bring to birth. Circles three of water, life force flowing free, power to these crystals, healing may they be.

Psychic protection for yourself

Although your crystals do carry in-built protection, you would do well to protect yourself both before and after healing. This has the double effect of cleansing yourself and the area in which you have worked and closing down your energies so that they are not buzzing around in your head overnight. There are various methods available to you.

Smudging

Smudging, or smoke magic, is one of the most effective ways of protecting and cleansing an area in which you heal and also your own energy field and your crystals. You can use one of the traditional Native North American smudge sticks or bundles of dried and tied herbs. Smudge sticks are usually made of cedar or sagebrush (grey or white sage), which has much larger and broader leaves than culinary sage and grows in mountain and desert regions in America. They are widely available in New Age stores, some health-food shops and by mail order.

Sage is both cleansing and empowering, while cedar is purifying and healing. You can also use broad firm incense sticks in any of the purifying or protective fragrances listed below. Sandalwood or pine works especially well.

* Stand in the centre of the room and hold your smudge or incense stick in your power hand (the one you write with).
* Light the centre of your smudge stick and when it flares, blow it out and then gently blow upwards until the tip glows and you obtain a stream of smoke.
* Face each of the four cardinal directions and make clockwise circles, then raise your smudge stick upwards. This represents the fifth direction in the Amerindian world, that of Father Sky. Finally,

bring your stick vertically downwards to greet Mother Earth.

* Now smudge a large clockwise circle around yourself, saying:

    Above and around, protect and ground.

* Extinguish the stick either in sand or by tapping it against a heatproof ceramic surface.

* When you have finished your crystal healing, light your smudge once more and greet the six directions again, then swirl an anti-clockwise smoke circle around yourself. You can hold your crystals in a dish in your receptive hand (this is the one you don't write with) as you smudge or you can pass the smudge over them afterwards to cleanse them. You can also empower crystals by passing them nine times, first anti-clockwise and then clockwise, through the smudging flame.

Protective crystals

From the Ancient Babylonians, Egyptians and the world of the Orient, over the millennia certain crystals have acquired the reputation of possessing strong protective qualities. They are usually also potent in strengthening and healing.

These include amber, black agate, amethyst, bloodstone, carnelian, garnet, jade, black and red jasper, jet, lapis lazuli, tiger's eye, topaz and turquoise.

You can place protective crystals at the corners of your healing altar or in the four corners of the room in which you are healing. Visualise them, if you like, as shadowy guardians or as angels of light guarding you as you work. On the whole, it is better to keep these specifically for protection and use other crystals for healing.

You will need to rest these crystals regularly. Wrap them in dark silk with a large piece of unpolished amethyst for a few days, taking care not to scratch them. You can revive the amethyst periodically by leaving it in a rainstorm or burying it in a large pot of healing herbs for 48 hours, then brushing off the soil and rinsing it in running water.

Incenses and oils

You will already have noticed that in some rituals I suggest using incenses and oils. These can increase the power of your crystal healing. As with crystals, you can choose those you feel a particular affinity for, or select them for particular purposes. Incenses tend to give a more instant effect, while oils are more subtle, with a gradual build-up of energies.

Basil, for growth and abundance

Basil brings increase in all things – health, love, prosperity – and is excellent for rituals of regeneration for the environment. Deeply protective, basil drives away all harm.

Bay, for health and fidelity

Bay will maintain and promote good health and trust and faithfulness in relationships. It offers psychic protection, heals sorrow and purifies all forms of pollution and negativity. It is good for rituals to heal the planet.

Chamomile, for gentleness and for use with children

This is a good herb for deflecting anger or hostility and for protecting children. It brings abundance and prosperity, family happiness and the growth of trust after betrayal and loss. It is also protective and deters those who would do harm.

Fennel, for courage and protection
Fennel is effective in repelling negative energies and brings the courage to stand up for principles. It offers protection from unwanted visitors and all forms of external hostility.

Frankincense, for power and higher energies
Frankincense eases tension, slowly replacing exhaustion with new optimism. An incense and oil used in many cultures to appease the gods and drive away dark spirits, frankincense was regarded as a gift of the gods that could cure all known ills. It helps connection with angels and one's higher or evolved self.

Juniper, for cleansing and marking boundaries
Juniper is traditionally a protector against accidents, psychic forces, violence and sickness. It heightens psychic awareness and guards the home and family against misfortune.

Lavender, for balance and harmony
Lavender restores balance and creates a peaceful atmosphere. It has calming and restorative properties, promises a gradual and gentle improvement in health, encourages gentle, positive interactions and brings love.

Mint, for uplifting and cleansing
Mint protects travellers and is a healing and purifying herb at home and in sickrooms, where it drives away all negativity and illness.

Myrrh, for regeneration and new beginnings
Another sacred oil and incense, myrrh symbolises healing, especially of sorrow and grief. It also connects with angelic wisdom and brings wisdom, understanding and compassion.

Patchouli, for joy and altruism
A symbol of peace and happiness, patchouli is used in 'green' rituals to heal the environment. It also brings increase in every way.

Pine, for purification and protection

Pine, fir and spruce can all be burned to cleanse away negativity and repel dishonesty, psychic attack or stress caused by emotional blackmail. They also offer the courage to continue on a difficult path and are effective in amplifying the effects of all healing. Pine is very protective, returning hostility to the sender.

Rose, for forgiveness and self-esteem

Roses bring love and especially the restoration of self-love and esteem, while also increasing psychic awareness. They offer gentle healing of mind, body and spirit and are especially potent for healing any form of abuse.

Rosemary, for healing and clarity

Rosemary, also known as elf leaf, brings clarity of mind and enhances energy levels. It is a herb of protection, healing illness and malaise, driving away bad dreams and offering consolation and courage in destructive or confrontational relationships.

Sandalwood, for peace and intuition
Sandalwood is another sacred oil, bringing harmony and balance, relieving nervous tension, fears and depression and bringing love. It increases psychic awareness and is very protective.

Thyme, for health and clear focus
Thyme is a health-bringer, improving memory and increasing concentration. It also endows courage and strength, keeps away bad dreams and increases psychic powers. It purifies of all forms of negativity.

Chapter 3
Beginning crystal healing

Healers throughout the ages have spoken about the healing touch. This contact, whether through the fingertips, the voice, the mind or all three, is the key to all kinds of healing, including healing with crystals. Some regard it as the connection between the transmitter force – the healer – and the higher energy, which is amplified by the crystal. If a recipient is receptive and willing to be healed, the process will be far easier. Young children and animals are particularly good recipients, as their psychic energy fields are very open to healing energies. When you send healing to a place, you are releasing the energies in a natural environment that will absorb the rays as part of the constant interchange of energies.

Few healers would claim to work without the aid of a higher force, be this a deity, an Archangel, a spiritually evolved nature spirit called a Deva or the life force in its purest highest form. Even healers without a conventional religious faith often visualise this healing power in terms of angels or light.

While drawing out pain or darkness, many healers nevertheless focus primarily not on the illness but on the state of wholeness and health of the patient that is the desired end result of healing. However, in spite of some miracle cures, there are times when the aim of healing is the temporary relief of pain and uplifting of the spirit. You should not, even with the best intentions, promise permanent cures or instant happiness, even if you know it is what the recipient wants most in the world.

Intuitive healing

As I said earlier, we all have the ability to heal quite instinctively, and crystals focus and amplify these innate energies as they mingle with the crystals' own restorative powers. These can be enhanced with the use of chakras, the psychic energy points in the body. Before the creation of the Theosophical movement in 1875, which brought the philosophy of the Far East into Western consciousness, few people in the West had any knowledge of chakras and their effects on the auric field. Such information can be very helpful as one way of understanding the flow of energy within the body and how crystals can ensure the free flow and purity of this energy.

There is great disagreement, even among experts, about the number and location of these energy points, which does lead to some confusion. I have not introduced auras and chakras in relation to crystal healing until Chapter 7, as I think it is important first to learn to trust your instinctive healing wisdom. Once you have felt or sensed the bodily flows of spiritual energy, then you can decide whether and how the chakra symbol system can be used to add to what you already know on this intuitive level. After all, there were many fine healers in the West pre-1875, often uneducated country people who healed with their hearts.

When you begin healing either yourself or loved ones using crystals, you may 'feel' or perhaps visualise the healing energies as warm liquid beginning in your heart and flowing into your hand and the crystal. This is, of course, a two-way process, and the powers are also coming from the crystal into your heart and being recirculated via the hand back through the crystal and into the patient.

This process is sometimes called 'contact healing' because the patient is present and involved in the process and the energies are transmitted directly via the crystal from the healer to the recipient. Self-healing also falls into this area.

Despite the word 'contact', which I have used several times, in all crystal healing you work with the person fully clothed, although he or she may prefer to take off shoes and any restricting items. We all have different levels of acceptable intimacy, but unless children are your own, and certainly with members of the opposite sex, it may be easier to confine direct touch to the hands, head, face, neck, back and feet.

In fact, since contact crystal healing is a spiritual process involving psychic energies, you may achieve greater spiritual closeness if you do not invade the physical space of the patient. In Chapter 4, I describe healing using a crystal sphere, for which you and the patient hold the crystal at the same time, which I think is a perfect compromise between intimacy and maintaining personal physical space.

Tracing the bodily energy channels

You can intuitively trace your own energy lines and perhaps identify psychic energy centres using either a pendulum or a clear crystal quartz. If you use this method for healing other people, you may notice that these energy points are quite similar in a number of patients, and when you read Chapter 7 you will realise that you have already identified the main chakra points.

As well as tracing your energy paths, the crystal restores natural harmony as it moves.

* Beginning at the level of the base of your spine, trace an 'energy' path upwards through your body to your head.

* Hold the crystal or pendulum loosely in your power hand, the one

you use for writing, a short distance away from your body.

* Let it swing to and fro, from your back at the base of your spine to your reproductive organs. The pendulum may swing gently in a clockwise direction, and if you are holding a crystal you may sense or feel physically a gentle vibration or buzzing.

* Move your hand slowly up the front of your body, allowing the crystal to trace its own path. If the pendulum ceases to swing or the crystal stops vibrating, this means you have lost the energy source. Retrace your path to where you last felt it.

* Relax and let your crystal or pendulum move when and where it is ready. It is being controlled not by your conscious mind but by the deep innate wisdom that is connected with the psychic energy within you.

* The pendulum or crystal may spiral at spots throughout your body, as though it was encountering a small whirlpool. This is a chakra or an energy point through which power flows through the body and into your aura – your personal energy field that encloses you. You may feel similar power surges in the areas of the main internal organs. For example, directly over the heart, the sensation has been described as a warm vibrating drum beat.

* If the pendulum or crystal feels heavy, seems to vibrate out of rhythm or becomes stuck, this may indicate an energy blockage point or a psychic knot. If you encounter a knot or blockage, circle the crystal or pendulum gently anti-clockwise until you feel the tension loosening.

* Continue to follow the path until you reach the crown of your head.

Carry this out every week or after major stress or a minor illness and you can keep your body energy flowing clear. You can also use this method on friends and family.

Afterwards, cleanse your pendulum or crystal by plunging it into clear water, preferably in sunlight, shaking off the water and allowing it to dry naturally. This action will empower as well as cleanse it. Alternatively, use one of the methods listed on pages 37–40.

You might like to keep this diagnostic healing crystal in a small velvet pouch separate from your other healing crystals.

Healing with your pendulum or clear quartz crystal

If you experience pain or discomfort in a particular area, you can use a pendulum or crystal quartz to give relief. You will note that anti-clockwise movement is used to remove pain and clockwise movement to restore energy to the affected area.

* Circle your pendulum or crystal in an anti-clockwise direction over the area.

* Visualise the pain or discomfort rising as a dark mist or a piece of grey knotted wool that the crystal tugs until it is free and forms a long wispy strand.

* Cast the strand mentally into the cosmos to form a star or a sunbeam.

* Rotate the crystal or pendulum clockwise over the spot to replace the pain with healing energies, seeing pure white light energy pouring through the crystal into the body.

* If it still does not feel right, allow the crystal to lead you in its spiralling pathway to another part of the body, where you may sense that there is a tangle. This may be in an area that comes as a surprise – frequently, for example, allergies or headaches may have a source in the stomach, and general infection may stem from a swollen gland.

* Untangle this spot and visualise the pain or discomfort being replaced with white light.
* Continue to let the pendulum move. It may lead you to two or three spots before the problem is resolved.

Do not try to second-guess or rationalise the process. Crystal healing is, as I said in the Introduction, the art of merging with your crystal and allowing it to direct your hand and healing energies.

If you lose concentration or experience sudden doubts about your ability – which many of the best healers do – just close your eyes, visualising stars in a velvet sky going out one by one until there is darkness and peace within. Then with your eyes closed, following the inner crystal light, begin again until you have re-established the inner rhythm.

Intuitive healing using pairs of crystals

There are a number of very effective ways of using pairs of crystals both to set up a healing energy circuit within yourself or a recipient and to balance the energies in the body.

Once again, this is largely an intuitive process, somewhat like learning to listen to a car engine when changing gear rather than looking at the speedometer.

Crystalline recycling

This is a fairly energy-intensive form of crystal healing, so you should protect yourself beforehand, perhaps by taking a bath to which a few drops of protective oils such as rose, ylang-ylang or geranium have been added. Then you should either smudge (see pages 40–1) or breathe in the light of an amethyst to enclose yourself in a circle of purple light (see Chapter 8 for more examples of crystalline psychic protection in the everyday world).

Afterwards you should again smudge and then press down hard with your feet on the ground, allowing excess energies to flow away and be re-absorbed by Mother Earth.

Use two virtually identical crystals, for example a pair of clear crystal quartz, one of which introduces crystalline life force energies to the body of the patient and the other of which extracts stale energies. For gentler healing, use a pair of rose quartz or amethyst. If the patient is feeling depressed, try two matching citrines.

The energies will be circulated through your hands and body and regenerated by the first crystal in a continuing cycle. You use either the patient's feet or hands as the two termini.

This is also a good way of recycling your own energies and in this case is entirely empowering. You just need to modify the method slightly.

If possible, work in sunlight or, if you are working after dark, surround yourself and the recipient with three or four pure beeswax candles at a safe distance.

* Hold the crystals, one in each of your hands, and with your power hand gently press one of the crystals into the recipient's opposite foot (so, for example, use your right hand with his or her left foot).
* If you are using hands, then cross your hands and ask the patient to hold the end of the crystal in your right or power hand to their left. As you are the transmitter, it is your power hand that is the crucial one, even if the patient is left-handed.
* Visualise the light flowing through the crystal and getting brighter and clearer, then flowing through the connected hand or foot of the patient.
* Allow the energy to find its own channels to the crown of the head. As you relax, it will flow out of the opposite hand or foot, passing through your body and in again.

Two or three minutes of this kind of healing for other people is sufficient.

Balancing the energies

Sometimes you or the person you are healing may feel that one emotion or aspect of being is predominating, perhaps an urge for constant activity and an inability to relax that can lead to burn-out and insomnia. Alternatively, you or the person you are healing may feel constantly anxious or too easily moved to tears or anger and this free-floating anxiety can interfere with concentration. Generally, these imbalances have an identifiable cause, such as a betrayal, a loss, an increased workload or an actual hormonal imbalance, for example during the menopause or pregnancy.

Pairs of crystals are very effective for healing this kind of condition by providing balancing energies to restore emotional equilibrium. They have the added advantage that, unlike herbs and oils, they are entirely safe for young children, pregnant women and people with allergies or breathing difficulties. This is because they operate on the psychic and spiritual levels, but since the whole system is interconnected, any improvements will be felt in body, emotions and mind. Under normal circumstances, when practising energy balancing, the crystals are applied directly to the skin. However, if you do not know the person very well, you can, if you prefer, hold the crystals close to but not touching the body.

Choosing your crystal pairs

If you have any doubts about which crystal pairs to use, then place all your healing crystals in a drawstring bag and, allowing your mind to go blank, feel in the bag. Take as much time as you need to select the two appropriate crystals. Do not be surprised or try to override this unconscious selection, for it draws on factors beyond the conscious mind. As with any psychic selection, such as selecting the right Tarot cards to answer a specific question, you are tapping into psychokinetic processes whereby the mind at a very deep level influences the crystal you choose to offer healing.

As I mentioned in the Introduction, a child can instinctively select the right crystal without hesitation, but adults, who are versed in logic, need to make sure that we pick *without looking*, to block the physical senses that are driven by logical considerations.

Some healers, myself included, will often ask the patient to use this unconscious selection process to choose 'their' crystals. When working with strangers at healing festivals, I have frequently discovered that a person who draws two crystals without looking from my own very extensive bag of more than 150 different crystals will then produce identical crystals from their own pocket or bag that have personal significance.

I like to use amber and a blue lace agate for personal healing. I find that they offer a balance of harmony with power. In addition, I have worked successfully with the following pairs on a number of occasions. In each case, the first has energising powers and the second soothing and protective powers.

Amber or carnelian/blue lace agate
For a steady flow of energy, but also the ability to rest.

Red and orange-banded agate/jade:
To relieve intense trauma and encourage gentle regrowth.

Citrine/moonstone
For solar and lunar energies, to bring the restoration of natural rhythms after a period of change or overwork.

Clear crystal quartz/smoky quartz
For recovery after chronic or severe illness or loss.

Clear or lavender fluorite/rose quartz
A gentle combination for children, old people or anyone who has been feeling vulnerable and prey to fear.

Green malachite/kunzite
For strength and courage after abuse or an exhausting situation that cannot be alleviated.

Healing with your crystal pairs
You can use the circuit method described on pages 53–4 with the matching pairs, applying the energising crystal with your power hand.

Alternatively, beginning near the base of your spine, move the crystals on parallel courses, so that they spiral and cross over like snakes curled around a stick. This is the way the body channels are sometimes portrayed in Far Eastern philosophy and resembles the healing rod or caduceus of Hermes the Greek god of healing and his Roman counterpart Mercury.

Before you start trying to release healing energies, practise moving the crystals at the same time, the first one in your power hand circling clockwise, and the second one in your receptive hand, moving anti-clockwise.

If you allow your instinctive wisdom to guide you, the crystals will increase movement in the area of the psychic power points and internal organs.

The dual action is in itself both healing and empowering, balancing the energies as the crystals move. Sometimes one stone will seem to be more active as the energies balance out.

If you encounter resistance, this indicates blocks in the energy flow, stagnation or psychic knots of tension, disease or discomfort. If this happens, allow the crystals to move in their own way to resolve the problem and then continue on their path.

After two or three passes up and down the body, the crystals will slow down and at this point balancing is complete.

Stand quite motionless for a minute or two as the energies finally align and the crystals cease to vibrate.

This method is by no means as exhausting as circuit healing, but remember to wash your stones. If you find that you are feeling tired, splash your hands and face with your sacred water and shake yourself like a dog to allow the healing water to flow around the psychic energy field that surrounds your body.

Whether you are healing yourself or someone else, you should do something to refresh yourself afterwards. If possible, go for a walk in the open air or eat fresh fruit, nuts and seeds or any unprocessed uncooked food to increase the flow of the life force within you.

Chapter 4
Healing with Crystal Spheres

Crystal spheres or balls, especially those made of clear crystal quartz, have a long healing tradition. In Ancient China, sunlight was directed through them on to a painful area of a patient's body. Sunlight and moonlight healing using spheres is very powerful. I describe techniques later in this chapter. Crystal balls are particularly effective for one-to-one healing, especially where there is emotional or spiritual distress or unresolved anger or guilt, and if you are an inexperienced healer, the sphere offers additional protection against depleting your personal strength because of its concentrated energy.

Choosing a crystal sphere

Your crystal sphere, or ball, need not be very large or expensive, but it should be pure crystal and not glass. It can also be used for divination. Clear crystal spheres are the most usual, and if you can find one with inclusions – small clusters of quartz – within, it will be especially potent. Some healers describe these inclusions as angels within the crystals. They are a good focus for people who are unfamiliar with crystals as they help to invoke healing images as you work.

Amethyst spheres are also very good for healing work; I have one that has many crystal inclusions within it. I have also seen quite beautiful spheres of rose quartz – another stone associated with healing. These last two work especially well in conjunction with moonlight and for gentle and gradual removal of pain or sorrow. Some healers like to use a clear crystal sphere for energising and for work with sunlight, as well as an amethyst or rose quartz ball for gentler, calming work.

Occasionally you find polished citrine spheres; these also work well in sunlight. For divination work, on the whole, the darker blue beryl crystal balls are best.

If possible, avoid buying your healing sphere by mail order. It is best to buy in person, so that you can try holding several to see which feels right for you; crystal balls that appear identical can actually have very different vibrations. So if a shop is pressing you to buy a particular – and expensive – ball, or is unwilling to let you take the time to hold a number of balls, go elsewhere.

Charging your sphere

The process of charging and cleansing crystal spheres is slightly different than that for smaller crystals because the larger ones emit such power and so can rapidly become depleted. You may wish to cleanse a new ball before charging it with your personal power, although the charging also purifies it of any negativity.

You will need Moon water and Sun water for this process. Moon water is made by placing spring water in a bowl outdoors on the night of the full moon so that it will absorb the light, appearing silver. Collect your Sun water by placing a clear crystal bowl of still mineral water in the open air to be infused with sunlight from dawn till dusk. The most powerful day of the year is the summer solstice, which falls around 21 June (21 December in the southern hemisphere), but any sunny day will do. As the water turns golden in the sunlight, stir it nine times clockwise (in the direction of the Sun) with a pointed, clear crystal quartz. Store your Sun water in clear glass bottles with a lid or stopper to use for cleansing and empowering your crystals.

* After dusk light a ring of small pale blue candles (blue is the colour of healing) around your crystal sphere.

* Breathe in the blue light through your nose very slowly and gently and then exhale it on to the surface of the crystal.

* As you do this, mentally invite an angelic or protective guardian to enter, empower and protect your sphere.

* Visualise a blue radiance or an angel or guide entering the crystal.

* Breathe on it nine times, seeing the angel growing brighter and clearer with each breath.

* Now empower the crystal by sprinkling it first with nine drops of Sun water and then nine drops of Moon water, saying:

Power of the Sun, Light of the Moon, enter this sphere, empower, guard and guide that I may work with pure heart and good intent.

Cleansing your sphere

When you have used your ball for healing, you will need to cleanse it.

* Rub it gently anti-clockwise with a white silk cloth or scarf, sprinkle it once more with nine drops of Sun and Moon water and leave it to dry naturally.

* When it is dry, rub it clockwise with the cloth. Wrap the crystal in the silk when not in use.

If someone is really ill or unhappy, use the following method for cleansing yourself and the ball after healing.

* Light a sage smudge stick or myrrh, pine or rose incense stick and, holding the ball in one hand, make nine anti-clockwise circles around the ball and yourself.

* Begin above the crown of your head and go down to your feet in spirals of smoke, followed by clockwise, upwards circles, and finishing with a smoke circle around your head.

Clockwise smoke circles around yourself and your ball are also a good form of extra psychic protection before healing work with your sphere if you know a session will be stressful or particularly intense (see also pages 40–1).

Healing using sunlight and your sphere

Sunlight is good for energising and improving physical health and vitality, ameliorating acute conditions, encouraging regrowth and regeneration in body and mind, and alleviating depression, sorrow, grief and fear. Use clear crystal quartz or citrine, being careful that the crystal does not get too hot. Work if possible when the sunlight is clear and bright.

You can use sunlight healing even if the Sun is not visible, for example on a dark, cloudy day or if you have to work at night. Just light golden candles, the colour of the Sun, around your sphere, and use extra golden coins or jewellery and mirrors to reflect the light.

Warning: Never look directly at the image or reflection of the Sun in the sphere as it can damage your eyes.

* Place your sphere on a table on which you have set a gold, red, orange or sunshine yellow cloth that will reflect into the sphere.

* Surround your sphere with yellow flowers, yellow or orange crystals, gold jewellery and coins, tiny mirrors, golden or orange fruits, seeds and nuts or dishes of herbs of the Sun such as rosemary, chamomile, St John's wort and bay.

* Lift the sphere in your power hand, up towards the light so that rainbows and golden light are reflected in the glass.

* Visualise this light as a guardian angel. The angel may be nameless, or you may prefer to call on the power of St Michael, the Archangel of the Sun, in his flaming gold and scarlet robes, to aid in your sun healing. Visualise his golden halo expanding to fill the crystal and brilliant rays radiating in all directions within and beyond the glass.

* Turning the sphere now to the person to be healed, focus first on the crown of the head, directing the light towards the painful part of the body. Gently revolve the sphere so that it does not become too hot.

* Slowly circle the ball in spirals up and down the body for general increase of health, confidence, joy and energy. Watch the sunbeams reflecting from it on the ceiling and walls if you are working indoors, or on the trees, bushes and flowers outside.

* Speak softly if you wish, chanting a mantra, for example:

  Sun power, Sun hour, radiant healing light, Sun shower, empower,
  with thy radiant sight.

* The power of the voice is also a source of healing energy and, especially if your subject is nervous, your words can help to open the channels whereby they can absorb the healing. Alternatively, you can allow words to flow about golden meadows, sunlit waters, warm beaches of soft golden sand, rainbows and sunbeams dancing in the clear blue air. As you create a golden scene, you can talk of the healing light flowing, the pain ebbing away, energy, joy, promise restored, of happy times ahead, increase, and abundance in every aspect of life. As I will describe later in the chapter, this talking therapy is amplified through the crystal sphere. I have found it far more effective than working in silence.

* After two or three minutes, if you look at the aura around your patient's head (see pages 114–16), you will notice that it is becoming lighter and clearer. After about five minutes, there should be subtle golden or white light, like a faint halo. This means that the energies have entered the body and mind. At this point you can stop.

You can also use this same technique to give yourself energy and restore optimism.

As you work, breathe in the golden radiance through your nose very gently and exhale darkness through your mouth. Establish a rhythm in your breathing and continue until you have exhaled all the darkness and you can see in your mind's vision that only clear light remains.

Healing with moonlight and your sphere

Moonlight is potent for removing illness or pain, for chronic or psychosomatic illnesses and for soothing and melting tension and anxiety or hyperactivity. Use clear quartz, amethyst or rose quartz. Full moonlight is most potent of all. Waxing energies will gently improve health, waning energies will lessen the power of addictions and compulsions. Work when the Moon is bright so that its silver light fills the sphere. If you are using a coloured sphere, for example a purple amethyst, it should filter through in a crystalline circle.

If the Moon is not visible in the sky, substitute a circle of silver candles as the source of light and add tiny silver mirrors, jewellery and coins to reflect the light.

* Place the ball on a cloth of silver or white and surround it with white flowers, moonstones or pearly crystals, fruits containing a lot of water, silver coins or jewellery and herbs of the Moon such as myrrh, jasmine, mimosa or eucalyptus.

* With your receptive hand, hold the sphere towards the light so that it reflects silver moonbeams.

* Visualise the light as a guardian angel. Gabriel is the Archangel of the Moon and he can assist your angel within the crystal. Visualise him in robes of silver, green and blue entering the sphere and the silver radiance spreading within and beyond the sphere.

* Beginning at the heart, direct the light towards the area of discomfort in anti-clockwise circles (the direction of the Moon), drawing out all that causes distress or is no longer of value and replacing it with silver healing light. Alternatively, spiral the ball from the heart upwards and then down so that it catches the moonbeams.

* Chant a mesmeric mantra, for example:

Moon of silver, gentle glow, take away all pain, sorrow, healing light, thus bestow.

* Alternatively, create in words a moonlit scene that your patient can imagine. Speak of silver pathways across the sea, the full Moon reflected in a deep lake, magical forests tinged with light, a huge orange Moon rising over the fields, bringing gentle restoration of tranquillity, peaceful dreams and spiritual wisdom as all that is dark or brings pain is carried out on the glittering waves.
* Look at the aura of the person you are healing. It will be silver, filled with stars and shimmering lights.

If you are healing yourself, use the same technique. Breathe in the light and breathe out the darkness until there is only a single star of light in your mind's eye, of which you are the centre.

Transmitting healing energies with your crystal sphere

I used this technique with some success at recent healing festivals in Sweden. It works especially well with people who have suffered prolonged or debilitating illnesses or who have experienced a major emotional crisis that has left them lacking confidence. It combines clairvoyance, counselling and healing, and, most importantly, triggers the innate self-healing powers of the patient as well as a greater self-awareness of their own potential strengths and the possibilities open to them on many levels.

Once again, because this is a very personal and intimate form of healing, it is important to make sure that you protect yourself spiritually before beginning (see pages 40–5), as you can otherwise absorb the pain and sorrow of the person who is being healed. Smudging is especially effective for guarding your own aura from any negativity that is shed (see page 40).

✳ Light lavender or rose incense and a silver, pink or purple candle.

✳ Sit facing the person you are healing and place the crystal sphere on the table between you. I find that either clear crystal quartz or amethyst is most powerful.

✳ Place your hands and those of the person to be healed on the ball so that your energies meet in the crystal.

✳ Begin by talking. Allow the patient to explain how they feel and what they hope is to be gained by the session.

✳ Extend the scope of the dialogue to long-term hopes and dreams and then gently encourage them to pour out their fears, doubts and anxieties to be absorbed by the crystal sphere.

✳ Have ready a dish of cut threads in dark colours. If the problems are complex or deep, ask the patient to tie a knot in a thread and burn it in the candle flame, at the same time naming a fear or guilt. As he or she burns the thread, the following words can be spoken by both of you:

Tangle the anger, tangle the pain, by this flame make me free again.

✳ Burn as many threads as are needed. Between each burning, you should both make contact with the ball again.

✳ When all the negativity has been named and burned, ask the person being healed to keep holding the ball. Tell them to close their eyes and visualise the healing light flowing in a continuous circuit from the ball through the fingertips of their power hand, upwards through the hands and the arms, round the heart, upwards through the throat and eyes, right up to the head, then circulating down again to the feet and returning to the ball through their hand.

* As this is happening, speak words to create a healing visualisation, touching the sphere as you speak. This time the scenario may be more clairvoyant, leading into a brighter tomorrow. If you empty your mind of conscious thought and allow the images, sounds, fragrances and feelings to flow, the words will be quite spontaneous and usually inspiringly prophetic. Do not worry if the client shows emotion, as this is part of the healing process. The joint visualisation is transmitted through the medium of the crystal and the other person may add details. Tell them that they are welcome to do so. The visualisation may include many symbols, animals, birds, butterflies, mountains and seas and you may both experience sounds and fragrances, as these psychic creations are multi-sensory.

* Gradually allow your words to cease and ask the patient to open their eyes when they feel ready. Sit together in silence, holding the sphere and gazing into the candle flame.

* After a minute or two of peaceful reverie, you can slowly reintroduce the everyday world, emphasising the importance of rest, patience and the need to move forward a step at a time.

* Suggest crystals that may be of help, perhaps a tiny crystal sphere for support at home, and demonstrate how to empower it (see pages 36–8).

* At this point you may see in your mind's vision or externally the person's angelic guide or spirit guardian, and by tactful enquiry you may find that the person is aware of a presence or has been told by a medium of a benign essence that watches over them.

Absent healing using a crystal sphere

Healing ceremonies can be carried out in a group made up of friends or family members of the sick person or a more permanent psychic awareness or healing group. You can take it in turns to lead the group, although you may find that certain members are especially gifted in particular forms of crystal healing.

This ritual can be adapted to heal an animal or bird, an endangered species or a place under threat, using pictures, maps or symbols.

Work as close as you can to 10 pm, the traditional healing hour. Before you begin, burn sandalwood, myrrh or cedar incense sticks in the room. The group can sit on cushions on the floor in a circle. In the centre of the circle, place a tall blue candle. In front of it place a photograph or symbol of the absent sick or distressed person and in front of that a clear crystal sphere so that the candle light falls on them both. Beside them, put a small flower or pot of healing herbs, such as lavender or chamomile, to be empowered by the light.

✳ Beginning with the person in the north of the group and moving clockwise, each member in turn lights a small pink or purple candle, stating what is for them the purpose of the ritual and their hopes for the patient. This need only be a few personal words to establish the connection with both the group and the absent person. For example, one of the group might say:

I light my candle for my dear friend Annie who is in hospital having an operation. I know she is frightened and so I send calming thoughts in the flame.

✳ As each member lights their candle and speaks, the leader of the group lifts the crystal sphere in both hands and takes it to them. Both momentarily touch the sphere, saying at the same time:

May the crystal circle of light remain unbroken and
so increase in power.

✳ Now pass the crystal sphere round the circle from hand to hand, so that at all times two people are making connection through it, and repeating:

May the crystal circle of light remain unbroken and
so increase in power.

✳ When the sphere has passed round the circle and is returned to the leader, raise it high above the central blue candle while the group chant softly in unison, faster and faster:

Go forth, increase and multiply, healing light intensify,
power of love to Annie fly.

* Continue until the chant reaches a climax, then the leader claps once. This is the signal for the candles to be blown out, to the cry of:

Blessings fly!

* The leader then blows out the central blue candle.
* Now visualise a cone of light extending round and being absorbed into the aura of the sick person, animal or place, as the aura becomes bright and golden.
* Sit in silence in the darkness, pressing your hands and feet into the ground to earth any excess energy that might otherwise make relaxation or sleep difficult later in the evening.
* The next day take or send the empowered flower or herbs to the patient as a symbol of the continuing healing.

Chapter 5
Crystal Healing with Colour

Crystals are categorised according to their colour as well as their type. In healing, the colour of the crystal is usually the preferred criterion for selecting the right stone to relieve particular ailments or states of mind.

Colour healing has a long history, since, because of their living energies, crystals are a particularly effective way of transferring the powers inherent in different colours, not only for physical healing but also for positively affecting the mind and spirit. The Babylonians called the healing power of light the 'medicine of the gods', and healing colours, especially as manifest in crystals, have been used for thousands of years in China and in the Ayurvedic medicine of India. The Ancient Egyptians, too, wore amulets of coloured stones: red to treat disease; yellow for happiness and prosperity, and green for fertility.

However, as you work increasingly with crystal energies, you may become aware that specific kinds of crystals do share common healing properties that are true regardless of their colour. For example, agates of every colour are used to balance emotions, and quartz crystals invariably cause a change in state of mind, whatever their colour. However, your choice of colour will affect the intensity of the power of the crystal. So, in the case of the quartz, if you want to effect a gentle change, you should use a soft pink rose quartz, whereas for a new beginning or to clear stagnation a clear crystal quartz would give a blast of energy.

Using colour in healing

Each of us has an aura, a psychic energy field within us and surrounding us that is made up of the colours of the rainbow. These colours are closely linked to the health of body, mind and spirit. By interpreting any problem through examination of the aura, it is possible not only to alleviate symptoms and the underlying cause but also to replace any pain, tension or exhaustion with the life force. You can infuse the whole system with light from an appropriately coloured crystal or use the light from a coloured crystal to add vitality to the body by circling it over the aura. Particular illnesses or malfunctions may be manifest as discoloration of, or an actual hole in the aura. You can also heal these by circling the crystal over the auric field above the head.

In the same way, water infused with coloured crystal energies is a way of boosting the system and driving away pain or tension. You may drink this energy-infused water or add it to your bath water.

In addition, you can supplement crystal colour power by burning a candle of the same colour while you are healing.

Colour meanings

It is being increasingly recognised in westernised industrial society that the state of spirit and mind can and do have a profound effect on physical health (indigenous societies have of course always known this). I have listed below the significance of colour on each of these three levels. Crystalline energies are a very effective way of healing on all three simultaneously. Note that sometimes you will need to use more than one colour.

I have given sub-headings under each colour meaning. The first, referring to the spiritual significance, addresses the effect of crystalline light on a person's spiritual development. I have then listed the positive qualities of the colour's energies, which represent the beneficial effects of the crystal colour. The negative associations are the problems indicated by an imbalance of the colour, whether a harsh tone, a lack of colour or discolouration (see pages 105–9 for how to distinguish these). I have also listed the crystals that seem to work especially well and are easily obtainable, although you may find others in the same colour that are better for you.

White or clear

Spiritual significance: Spiritual awakening, connection with the higher self or spirit/angel guides.

Positive qualities: The free flow of the life force.

Negative associations: Becoming out of touch with the real world, inability to operate effectively on the material plane.

Physical effects: Wholeness, health and healing, integration of mind, body and soul. White light is a natural pain-reliever and can help to protect against cerebral disorders, increase breast milk in nursing mothers, speed the mending of broken bones and relieve calcium deficiency and toothache. It also boosts energy levels.

Crystals: Diamond, clear fluorite, moonstone, clear crystal quartz, zircon.

Red
Red is for power and vitality.
Spiritual significance: Increases spiritual strength, helps people to face and overcome physical/material problems in a non-aggressive way.
Positive qualities: Energy, determination, impetus for positive change.
Negative associations: Becoming aggressive, domineering or angry for little reason.
Physical effects: Red stimulates the entire system and restores energy levels. It is good for raising blood pressure and improving circulation, promoting cellular growth and activity; red crystals are used in healing blood ailments, especially anaemia. Red light is linked to reproduction and fertility and relieves sexual dysfunction, especially impotence; it also helps with pains in the feet, hands, bones and back.
Crystals: Blood agate, garnet, jasper, ruby.

Orange
Orange is for confidence and self-esteem.
Spiritual significance: Brings insight and acceptance of own nature, both positive and negative.
Positive qualities: Enthusiasm, originality, creativity, independence.
Negative associations: Restlessness, poor self-image, idiosyncrasy.
Physical effects: Another colour of energy, fertility and warmth, orange eases arthritis, rheumatism, gall-bladder and kidney problems (including stones), menstrual and muscle cramps and allergies. It also increases the pulse rate and lifts exhaustion. Orange is used to strengthen the immune system.
Crystals: Amber, beryl, carnelian, jasper.

Yellow

Yellow is for happiness and knowledge of all kinds.

Spiritual significance: Learning what is of worth, having the will-power to follow the right path.

Positive qualities: Optimism, joy, focus.

Negative associations: Hyperactivity, selfishness, unpredictability.

Physical effects: Stimulates the nervous system, improving memory and concentration and easing eczema and skin problems. It also promotes a healthy metabolism and calms anxiety and stress-related ailments that may affect the digestive system adversely. Yellow may also be beneficial in the treatment of arthritis and rheumatism, eczema and skin problems.

Crystals: Calcite, citrine, rutilated quartz, topaz.

Green

Green is for peace and balance.

Spiritual significance: Connection with nature and devas or higher nature spirits, regeneration, integration.

Positive qualities: Peace of mind, love for others and for the environment.

Negative associations: Easily swayed by emotions and sentiment, unwillingness to stand alone.

Physical effects: Restorative for heart, lungs and respiratory system, green helps to fight infections and viruses, especially influenza, bronchitis, fevers and colds. It also counters panic attacks, addictions and food-related illnesses. Green is a good healing colour because it stimulates tissue and cell growth and general body regeneration; it also encourages fertility. Green is the colour for healing the Earth.

Crystals: Jade, malachite, emerald, tourmaline. **Warning:** Malachite can be poisonous if taken internally, so use another stone if healing small children or animals and do not add to water.

Blue

Blue is for idealism and wisdom. It is called the healing colour because a blue aura is often seen around healers.

Spiritual significance: Expansion of spiritual horizons, channelling higher and ancient wisdom.

Positive qualities: Altruism, healing powers, leadership.

Negative associations: Ultra-conservative attitudes, obsession with order and detail.

Physical effects: Blue is a natural antiseptic, soothing and cooling, relieving burns, cuts, bruises, insomnia, inflammation of the skin and mouth, sore throats and childhood rashes and teething pains. It also lowers high temperatures and high blood pressure. Blue is potent for healing air pollution and the seas. All shades of blue, such as violet and indigo, relieve migraines and headaches.

Crystals: Lapis lazuli, blue lace agate, sapphire, turquoise.

Purple

Purple is for inner vision and intuition. This includes all shades of purple from indigo through lavender to violet.

Spiritual significance: Looking inwards to the collective wisdom of mankind, unconscious wisdom.

Positive qualities: Inspiration and clairvoyant visions.

Negative associations: Inability to apply wisdom, naivety.

Physical effects: Some call purple the all-healer, for it relieves so many conditions, counteracting doubts and negativity; it is good against allergies, asthma, sleep disorders and stress-related illnesses. Purple eases eye, ear, nose and skin problems and migraines. It aids deep-tissue healing and mending of bones and is a natural sedative; it also helps neuroses and obsessions and eases childbirth.

Crystals: Amethyst, fluorite, sodalite, sugilite.

Pink

Spiritual significance: Expressing spiritual love through relationships.

Positive qualities: Patience, acceptance of human frailty, forgiveness of self and others.

Negative associations: Sentimentality, possessiveness.

Physical effects: The gentle healer, pink promotes restful sleep and pleasant dreams and encourages optimism. Pink relieves ear, eye and gland problems, head pains and psychosomatic illnesses, as well as all disorders relating to children and babies, especially fretfulness and hyperactivity.

Crystals: Coral, pink kunzite, rose quartz, tourmaline.

Brown

Spiritual significance: Connection with the Earth and awareness of the sanctity of all creation – stones, insects, plants and animals as well as humankind.

Positive qualities: Nurturing and protectiveness, especially of the vulnerable, animals and wildlife.

Negative associations: Materialism, lack of vision.

Physical effects: Brown grounds energies, absorbs pain and sorrow, increases physical energy and primal strength, and relieves disorders connected with feet, the legs, the hands, the skeleton, all back pain and also the large intestine. It is good for healing animals and the Earth.

Crystals: Desert rose, rutilated quartz, smoky quartz, tiger's eye.

Black

While not generally used in healing, dark grey or black stones are very protective and can also be used to ease the passing of adults and for generally allaying grief.

Crystals: Obsidian (Apache tears), black jasper, smoky quartz, jet.

Dowsing

Dowsing is a scientifically accepted way of discovering water, oil, minerals or lost objects. It can be carried out by actually visiting a location, but this is not always necessary as you can use the method known as remote dowsing. To do this, hold a pendulum over a map or diagram of the area. The pendulum will make a clockwise positive swing, or pull downwards and feel heavy over the precise location of the thing you are seeking.

Dowsing with a crystal pendulum is a valuable way of fine-tuning your crystal healing and can be used to establish not only the site of the problem but also exactly which crystal colour to use to treat it. We have already seen how to choose the colour of crystal (see the colour meanings on pages 73–4). However, if you know that, for example, you need a yellow crystal for a digestive problem, you could set out two or three different kinds of yellow stones and ask the pendulum to indicate which is best to alleviate the specific condition.

Using a pendulum for remote dowsing

If you do not know the precise nature of an illness or distress, or suspect that there may be a number of related areas, draw a rough outline of the body (this may be either your own body or that of the person to be healed).

* Move the pendulum slowly over the picture asking it to show you the location where healing would be helpful. It may circle or pull down as if being dragged by gravity either over a single area or a number of places. You will usually find that these areas are connected.
* Now fine-tune this knowledge by asking which colours will heal each of the areas.

* Write a list of the problem spots and go through them in turn. The information revealed may be surprising but is usually accurate.
* To find the colour needed for each ailment, draw a circle divided into nine segments, each one representing one of the colours listed above, excluding black. You can colour each segment appropriately or write the name of the colour. If you draw the circle on stiff card and laminate it, you can use the chart for other crystal healing. Alternatively, you can pass your pendulum over a circle of nine different coloured crystals.
* Pass your pendulum over the diagram or crystals, so that it can select the colour needed. It will indicate its choice either by a positive circling or by pulling down over the best colour for healing that place.

So, for example, your pendulum might when held over the diagram of the body locate the problem spot around the root of the spine, which would indicate that the source of any back pain or tension was due to pressure right at the base.

However, the healing colour that the pendulum chose on the colour chart might be pink, rather than the usual dark red or brown associated with that area of the body. This might indicate that the pain was psychosomatic, possibly due to family tension or unresolved emotional pain causing the patient to hold their body rigid to avoid revealing their feelings.

So while simple colour meanings are a good guide to the best crystal to choose, if you feel intuitively that there is more to the situation than meets the eye, it is a good idea to dowse for a more precise indication of the right colour.

Crystalline water

One of the most effective ways to absorb the positive effects of crystals and their colours is by drinking crystalline water. This is powerful not only when you need healing but also to maintain well-being.

Making crystalline water is quite simple. Make separate coloured waters on different days and store each in a bottle of the appropriate colour. As you make the water, sit in the light of the same colour candle as the crystal and gaze into it, endowing the crystal with any special wishes you have for its use or asking the crystal guardians to protect and empower it. Begin in the early morning if possible, just as it is getting light. You can blow out the candle as natural light filters through.

* Half-fill a crystal bowl with pure, still, spring water, if possible from a sacred source. Water from a number of these former holy springs is now bottled commercially, for example, Malvern water (the favourite of Queen Elizabeth II).

* Keep the bowl in the open air if possible, covered with fine mesh to prevent pollutants entering.

* Place flowers, plants, fruits or vegetables of the same colour around the bowl of water and add to the water two or three small or one larger crystal of the chosen colour and kind.

* Leave the water open for a full 24-hour cycle to absorb the power of the Sun and Moon. It does not matter if you cannot see the Sun or Moon in the sky as their energies are still present. The waxing Moon cycle is best for making crystal water.

* At the end of the cycle, place the crystals you have used with an amethyst chunk to re-energise them.

* Pour the water into coloured bottles.

Some people make the water directly in the bottles and leave the crystal in the water, but I prefer this method if you have time.

Uses of crystalline water

Specific crystalline waters may be used for particular problems.

Jade water: Traditionally brings long life and will improve and then maintain health, not only in people but also in animals. It is excellent poured on plants and into polluted rivers and seas to revitalise them.

Citrine water: Increases confidence and optimism as well as being good for digestion.

Agate water: Calms fears and prevents overreaction under provocation. Water empowered with a blue lace agate softens harsh words, so it is good for making coffee if difficult relations come to call.

Sodalite water: Helps to alleviate panic experienced when flying. Take a cloth moistened with it on to the aircraft; use this to dab your temples and pulse points on take off and landing or whenever you feel panic rising.

However, healing the body is only one small part of health; you should try to experiment with different uses for your infused waters and note any you find particularly effective. As with sacred water, take some colour-charged water to work or to a difficult social event in a mineral water bottle. You can also pour a little into a small flask or bottle and sip it or splash it on your wrists in times of stress or exhaustion. Add the appropriate crystal water to your bath for specific ailments or to uplift the spirits. You can even mix colours, by pouring a little into another bottle kept for special combinations. Make waters for specific occasions or people. Orange carnelian water, for example, is good for teenagers under stress at school or a first job and can be added to fruit juice or mineral water or put in breakfast coffee or tea. Though the water does not literally change colour, some people say they can see a faint aura round it.

Read through pages 74–9, where I listed the healing properties of the crystals, and then you can create water for almost every occasion. Make some in all the main nine colours, excluding black.

Traditionally, crystal water is kept in glass bottles of the same colour. Clear crystal quartz water can be kept in clear bottles. The bottles need only be small and you can obtain stained glass bottles with stoppers from many gift shops and from garage sales. Well-washed, empty bath-oil bottles are also good. You can keep your bottles of crystalline water in the fridge.

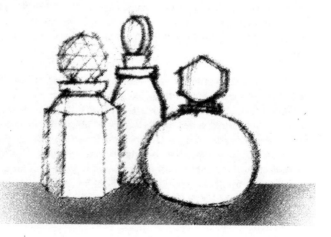

Crystal colour breathing

This method brings together breathing techniques and visualisation to help relaxation and to ease stress. When you need a boost of the healing energies associated with certain colours, you can visualise inhaling colour from a crystal just by holding a coloured crystal and gazing into it. You do not need to take huge breaths and it is quite possible to use this method very subtly even on a crowded train. You can touch the crystal in your pocket or bag as you visualise it in front of you.

This is a fast method of providing a sudden burst of energy or optimism to replace doubt or exhaustion or to calm down in a potentially explosive situation. You can also use this method for absent healing for a person, animal or place. It can be used to direct colour to a painful or disharmonious part of the body as well as for psychic protection and for cleansing the aura and chakras. Forms of psychic breathing are traditionally used to harness what is called *pranic* (or life force) energy. It can be used with other sources of colour, such as flowers, fruit or candles, but I find it most effective with crystals. If you find it difficult at first, add a coloured candle and place your crystal so that you can see the light shining through it.

* Breathe in slowly; hold this breath for a slow mental count of three ('One – and – two – and – three'), then exhale slowly through your mouth with a sigh. Do this five or six times.
* Visualise the air you are inhaling as the colour of the crystal radiating through your body.
* Exhale slowly, visualising black mist being expelled, leaving your body lighter and more harmonious.
* Slow your breathing a little more, picturing the coloured light

entering your lungs and spreading throughout your body.
* Hold your breath (count 'One – and – two – and – three').
* Breathe out slowly (count 'One – and – two – and – three'), once again expelling the dark mist.
* Use your exhaled breath to banish negative thoughts and your inhaled colour to introduce calm or energy. The warmer colours – red, yellow and orange – are stimulating and energising; the cooler colours – blue, green and purple – soothe and gently uplift.
* Once you are filled with light, make the colour you inhale the same as the one you exhale. It can now be used for healing.
* Continue to inhale and exhale gently. You can spread the light around your aura for power or protection or breathe the coloured energies towards a specific part of your body (looking in a mirror helps you to direct it). Alternatively, you can breathe the colour in your exhaled breath gently towards the patient.
* He or she can join in the breathing patterns and by visualising the light will not only be healed more effectively but also will be able to generate self-healing powers that will continue the effects between sessions.

* When you can visualise the aura (either that of your patient or your own if you are doing self-healing) filled with light, gently slow down the process until you are breathing quite normally. (See page 115 for an instant method of seeing auras.)
* Try to spend a few minutes gazing into the crystal, as after healing is often a time when quite profound clairvoyant insights are revealed not only to the healer but also through the psyche of the recipient if they are encouraged to talk. It is often at this time that they are able to provide answers to their own questions and make positive plans, however small, for the future.

This is one of the gentlest forms of healing. It can be used very effectively to banish night fears from children. Try inviting them to blow away the monsters of the day and night (and it's not a bad exercise for stressed adults!).

Chapter 6
Absent Healing with Crystals

n absent healing, energies are transmitted through a crystal to a sick or unhappy person who is some distance away. For though the rapport between healer and recipient is very powerful in a session when both are present, psychic energies can be sent even across continents with little dilution. In my 12 years of psychic research I have come across many accounts of people receiving telepathic messages from loved ones in a country thousands of miles away. Living ghosts, or spirit or etheric forms, which many believe are the part of us that survives death, do appear to a relative at moments of crisis, for example, during an operation or accident. At the point of actual bodily death, too, spirits of loved ones will span oceans to say goodbye. This was a feature of many paranormal contacts during the First and Second World Wars.

Using these same psychic channels, you can send love and healing light not only to friends and family but also to animals.

Crystal energies are a particularly powerful way of transmitting healing over a distance, whether from an individual healer or from a healing group (see the absent healing ceremony on pages 68–70). You can keep records of this in your healing book (see pages 28–9).

The ethics of absent healing

I have already mentioned the importance of asking the permission of the person you are healing. I think this is equally important when you are directing crystal energies by indirect means. These can include creating a representation of the person in a clay or cloth figure or a herb sachet. The ethics of such actions have been the subject of much discussion in healing circles. Some healers say that as long as you are sending positive love and thoughts, the effect can only be beneficial, and there is no need to inform the subject of your intentions. However, I do wonder whether illness and grief involve rather more complex questions. It is possible that in seeking to remove a condition without first asking permission we may be interfering with an unrecognised but interconnected process. Of course, no one wants to be ill or sad, but sometimes the body or mind malfunctions because of intense external or internal pressure. The period of illness or exhaustion can actually break a destructive cycle and may also offer a chance for reassessment.

In my own healing work, I have decided to compromise; when I am asked to send light and life to people I do not know, I always add the words 'if it is right to be' to any chant or prayer I use.

Choosing crystals for absent healing

You can use any of your healing crystals or a crystal sphere for absent healing. However, whether for group or individual work, I have found that pieces of unpolished amethyst, yellow, orange or green calcite, cloudy white crystal quartz and pink rose quartz are all very potent. You can buy large, unpolished pieces much more cheaply than the polished stones in a variety of sizes and I have found these to be very effective. You might like to buy a large piece for keeping on a table and smaller pieces to hold in your hand to direct energies. The properties of the unpolished chunks are identical to those of their more gleaming sisters, but they tend to be gentler in their energies and so are especially good for healing work for a patient over a period of time.

You can read about the properties of these crystals in Chapter 11, but I have described calcite in detail here.

Calcite for healing

Calcite in all its colours – which look like water ice – is good for absent healing. You might like to buy two or three colours. They are often obtainable in gift shops as well as the more usual New Age outlets, perhaps because they are relatively inexpensive – even large pieces.

You can choose from transparent or semi-transparent milky yellow, peach, green, white or clear crystals.

Calcite crystals are natural balancers of all energies of the body, mind and spirit, and so are good for restoring harmony to the system. They can be used for people, animals and even an ecosystem, and it does not matter if you are not certain of the dynamics of the illness or problem.

I have listed below the colours that are especially effective for healing. They are also effective in contact work with nervous patients.

Orange

Orange calcite is uplifting, restoring self-confidence and encouraging a return to normal life after a period of illness or depression. It is good for kidney problems, female disorders and for promoting fertility.

Blue

Blue calcite is a reliever of pain, especially in the back, and is good for all head, throat and neck problems, fears and a sense of isolation. It is also effective for cleansing the atmosphere, and for birds, the seas and sea creatures.

Green

Green calcite is a natural harmoniser and works well where there has been emotional or physical burn-out; it helps to prevent any recurrence of the same mistakes that led to the breakdown in health or harmony. It brings calm and helps to replace fears and destructive habits with positive ones. It clears toxins from the body and from places, and is good for land pollution or deforestation.

Yellow

Yellow calcite is another detoxification crystal, especially for the kidneys, pancreas, stomach and spleen and for decalcification of joints and bones. It is good for regenerating areas of industrial waste and for protecting urban developments and town-dwellers from negativity. It also eases anxiety, insomnia and hyperactivity.

White

Cloudy white calcite is very similar in appearance to cloudy unpolished quartz, though it is more balancing. It can be used for whole-body healing and by the gentle infusion of the life force can bring a gradual return to health and happiness.

Caring for your absent healing crystals

You should keep your unpolished crystals, especially calcite, very carefully, either on your healing table or wrapped separately in white silk so they do not crack or scratch other crystals. Unpolished chunks – even small ones – tend to have sharp points that are excellent for directing energies, but also for causing damage!

You can cleanse and empower your absent healing crystals using a crystal pendulum or any of the methods suggested on pages 36–9. You may also like to try the burying method I describe on page 42.

However, I find an infusion of sage, chamomile or peppermint especially good for crystals used in absent healing. All three herbs are natural healers, are protective and are readily available in herbal tea bags, which you can use to make an infusion. If you prefer to use unprepared ingredients, you will need one teaspoon (5 ml) of dried herbs or flowers for a bit less than one pint (500 ml) of water. If you are using fresh herbs or flowers, use three teaspoons (15 ml).

* Pour boiling water over the herbs in a pot and leave the infusion to cool.
* Strain the infusion into a ceramic or glass dish.
* Place your crystals on a ceramic plate or dish.
* Sprinkle nine drops of the infusion over the crystals and then make three protective clockwise circles of the herb water around the crystals. As you work, repeat nine times:

Take away all harm, take away all danger, bring light and healing to loved friend or stranger.

* Hold the crystals under running water to prevent them being stained. This acts both as cleansing and empowerment.

Beginning absent healing

This is primarily intended for someone you know. If you are healing a stranger, instead of visualising the person in detail, picture them framed in light so that their figure is in shadow. However, some healers say that when healing an unknown person, they do receive an image of the person that on later knowledge proves to be startlingly accurate. You can also use this method for an animal who is away from you. It is useful if your pet is having an operation or if you have had to leave it in a pet hotel and you know it will be pining.

Use two large, unpolished crystals, one either an uncut amethyst or rose quartz and the other a cloudy, uncut, crystal quartz, or white or yellow calcite. I have also successfully used this method with an unpolished amethyst and a clear crystal sphere.

* Place the two crystals side by side on a table.
* Behind the amethyst or rose quartz, light a pink or lilac candle, scented with rose or lavender.
* Face the direction in which the person lives or will be at the time of healing, visualising him or her in a particular place, indoors or in a garden.
* In your mind, build up a picture of the person in detail, including their voice and even their fragrance as well as their physical image.
* Holding the coloured crystal in both hands, visualise dark rays coming from the patient and entering the crystal, being transformed into circles of crystalline colour and floating like bubbles into the candle, where they are taken back as light.
* Return the crystal to the table.

* Using the coloured candle, light a pure white candle, perhaps scented with vanilla, and place it behind the white or yellow crystal or sphere.
* Pick up this second crystal. Let the light pass through it, forming a prism of rainbow colours, travelling to the sick person, entering through the crown of their head and filling their whole body with brilliance.
* Visualise a sparkling halo around the head of the patient.
* Return the crystal to the table.
* Leave the candles to burn through in a safe place in front of the crystals, so that the light from both will continue to filter gently for several hours towards the subject.

Using a crystal pendulum for absent healing

You can use this method even for strangers or for absent friends or family with complex illnesses or needs. On pages 49–51 I described how you could use a crystal pendulum over the diagram of a person to trace connections between problem areas of the body. In the same way, you can draw an outline to represent an absent subject and then infuse healing via the pendulum into the diagram.

Work in sunlight if possible. If not, light a ring of beeswax candles to create light beams in the pendulum.

* Draw the outline of a figure (or animal – this works just as well for them) and, as you do so, name the person to whom the healing will be sent.
* Ask the pendulum to indicate areas where there are problems. Slowly pass the pendulum over the diagram, beginning at the left foot and working upwards and then down again, ending at the right foot.

* If the pendulum circles anti-clockwise, this indicates a problem. If it appears to stick in a place, there may be a blockage. Alternatively, you may feel heaviness and the pendulum may pull downwards over the affected spot. If the movement is sluggish there may be a lack of energy flow at a particular point or if the sluggishness is more widespread a general exhaustion or depression. You may see obvious links but if not you can allow the pendulum to guide you.

* Mark all these areas and continue until the pendulum has finished indicating problem areas.

* Visualise the person once more and ask that healing light may be sent through the pendulum.

* Work once more over the figure, from the left foot upwards, pausing at any areas you marked and again allowing your unconscious wisdom to guide the pendulum as it swirls anti-clockwise, removing pain or stagnation. Sometimes you will find that over an area of the picture where the pendulum detected a lack of energies it automatically swirls clockwise to infuse power. But at other times it may seem to be tugging at a knot, changing direction until at last it settles.

* Flow with the movement, visualising the light beams travelling into the body of the recipient and the radiance spreading around them.

* When the pendulum becomes still, leave the diagram in the light of the Sun or the candles.

* Wash your pendulum under running water, then shake it dry.

Absent healing using an empowered clay figure

If you want to send healing over a period of time, perhaps for a chronic condition or one from which recovery is slow, you can create a more permanent, personalised symbol of the patient by using pure white clay to create a featureless figure.

* Decorate the figure with tiny clear crystal quartz and rose quartz crystals, naming the person and asking that the powers of goodness and light infuse the figure with healing.

* Place the figure on a small cushion and behind it, at a safe distance, light a pure beeswax candle. (You will not need this if the Sun is shining brightly.)

* Choose a crystal in a colour that relates to the illness if known. Otherwise, use your yellow, green, orange or white calcite or cloudy quartz if working by natural light, or the amethyst or rose quartz for candlelight. Circle the crystal three times anti-clockwise around the figure, saying:

Light of love, bring health and joy. Renewed strength, sorrow destroy.

* Then circle the crystal three times clockwise, saying:

*Healed in soul and mind and heart, darkness and pain now depart.
Gone is sorrow, gone is pain, strength and health alone remain.*

Alternatively, use your own words.

* Touch the head, the heart, the navel, the womb or genitals and the feet of the figure gently with the crystal, at each spot saying:

Heal and bless, you guardians of light, granting this if it is right.

* The last few words are my 'opt-out clause' to avoid taking over the free will of someone you have not asked permission to heal. However, you may wish to leave them out.

* Leave the figure and the crystal in the sunlight or until the candle has burned down.
* Wrap the figure in white silk and leave it on your healing altar, preferably next to a pot of healing herbs and ringed by crystals such as tiny rose quartz or clear crystal quartz for a more proactive approach.
* Repeat the ritual weekly.
* When the patient has recovered, bury the figure to return it to the Earth, planting some seeds as thanks for healing received.

Herbs for absent healing

You can focus additional power in your crystal healing by the use of healing herbs, usually packed into some kind of bag. Traditionally, empowered herbs were folded in small squares of coloured cloth, tied with three, six or nine knots of ribbon or twine of the same colour (see colour meanings on pages 74–9). Another method is to buy ready-made drawstring purses in different colours, as they make excellent instant herb pouches. You can also cut out two pieces of cloth in a doll shape, then join the two pieces at the feet, and fill the doll with the herbs before sewing up the head. This is called a 'poppet'.

Basil, chamomile, fennel, lavender, rose petals, rosemary, sage and thyme are all-purpose healing herbs suitable for using with crystals. However, the main healing power comes from the crystal energies with which you charge the herbs. (There are, of course, dozens of healing herbs, each with individual properties. See pages 188–9 for books listing them.)

This is how to empower your herbs.

* Place the dried flowers or herbs in a ceramic dish and again allow either natural sunlight or the light of a beeswax candle to fall on them.

* Using a pointed clear quartz crystal or your crystal pendulum, stir the herbs faster and faster, chanting:

Herbs of healing, fill with light, crystal power, crystal might,
Green light, herb power, healing shower; this I ask if it be right.

* Visualise green and white light pouring from Earth and sky into the herbs.

* With a final cry:

Earth and Sky power, at this hour, unite!

plunge the crystal into the herbs and then into a dish of sacred water, taking care not to splash the herbs.

* Fill the purse, cloth or featureless doll with the empowered herbs. If you wish, add one or two tiny rose or clear quartz crystals.

* Tie the cloth firmly or sew around the doll with running stitches of pure white cotton while repeating the chant.

You can place the herbal focus on your healing altar surrounded by tiny tubs of the chosen herbs and every night light a candle over it for a few minutes.

Absent healing in a group

Sometimes friends or family will want to gather together to pray for a sick friend or relative, or you may decide to form a healing group for a specific purpose. Perhaps, for example, you wish to send healing to war-torn areas or people or groups in your own community who need help. Sending light and love using crystals can also from part of more general psychic development group work (see pages 186–7 for training organisations for healing).

There are two ways in which you can work in a group with crystals. You may use a large central crystal as the focus, and pass it around a circle of healers. (I described this method using a crystal sphere on pages 68–72, and unpolished stones work just as well as a sphere.) Alternatively, as in the ritual given below, each healer can use an individual healing stone. This may be a personal polished stone or an unpolished calcite, amethyst or quartz that is small enough to be easily held.

A ritual to send healing to a war-torn land

Sit in a circle on cushions around a low central table covered with a pink cloth. On this table, place some of your large healing crystals and a horseshoe of three pale lilac candles. Do not light the candles. Burn rose or lavender incense sticks in a deep container. Use broad firm incense sticks with non-combustible handles so that they can be carried. Light a single large beeswax candle and if possible work after dusk on the waxing Moon. Each person should hold between his or her hands a healing crystal that has personal significance. The leader of the ritual will work with one of the large central crystals. Green calcite is very potent for this purpose

* One member of the group takes an incense stick from the central table and, beginning in the north, casts a circle of smoke around the group, saying:

I cast this circle of power and protection. May we work only with the highest intent for the increase of healing in – (name place to which the healing is to be sent).

* The member returns the stick to the container, which is then given to the person sitting in the north of the circle, and sits down.
* The incense container is passed round the circle. Each person in turn places it in front of them and passes their personal healing crystal through the smoke, saying:

Heal and bless our endeavour and – (name the place).

* When everyone has received the incense, the leader of the group returns the container to the table and passes his or her own large crystal through the incense, repeating the chant. Then he or she lights the first lilac candle and passes the crystal through the flame, saying:

I kindle this light that it may cross land and sea to heal the strife in which so many innocent people are suffering.

* Each of the group raises their own crystal, saying in unison:

Send peace, we ask, and reconciliation.

* The leader now lights the second candle and passes the large crystal through the first and second flames, saying:

The light grows. I kindle this light to fill the hearts of all who make war for the reasons they alone know. May it lead them to gentleness and reconciliation.

* The members raise their individual crystals in the direction of the central light, saying:

    Send consolation, we ask, to those who are wounded or who have lost their homes and families.

* The leader lights the third candle and passes the crystal in turn through all three flames, saying:

So love increases. I kindle this light to send consolation to those who are wounded or who have lost their homes and families.

* The members raise their crystals to the light and say:

    May life return and hope and joy, houses and crops and animals where now all is waste and devastation.

* Each person should then breathe in the crystalline light of their own crystal, sending healing thoughts and hopes for the future to the war zone.

* Finally the leader blows out each of the lilac candles in turn, saying:

    May life return.

* As the candles are extinguished, each member of the group projects crystalline light by exhaling softly three times, once for each candle.

* The group can sit in the light of the central beeswax candle and exchange ideas for practical contributions to ease the situation, whether writing letters, sending aid parcels or collecting donations.

* When the candle is burned through, the group can share a simple meal, prepared beforehand.

This ritual can be adapted for any joint healing purpose, or indeed for an individual healing ceremony, using only the leader's actions and words.

Chapter 7
Chakras and Healing Crystals

The chakras are the points on our bodies that receive and transmit energies between the body and its aura and the energy fields of other people, animals, plants, the Earth and the cosmos. These energies penetrate both the physical body and the spirit, or etheric, body. The etheric body is the essence that may survive death and, some believe, can move independently during out-of-body and near-death experiences.

Chakras are a vital concept in Hindu, Tibetan Buddhist and yogic traditions. They were first popularised in the West in the late nineteenth century by the Theosophical movement.

There are a large number of major and minor chakra points in the body, but western spirituality usually concentrates on seven main ones that correspond to the seven colours of the spectrum. The word *chakra* is Sanskrit for 'wheel', and the chakras that exist on the psychic rather than the biological level are usually pictured as whirling, multi-coloured circles, sometimes like lotus petals.

Because the chakras themselves do not exist on the physical level, they cannot be seen or measured, although Japanese experiments have demonstrated that energy levels of people who had worked with chakra energies over a period of years were discernably stronger, especially over the hypothesised chakra points, than those of a control group.

Most traditions locate the chakras along the vertical axis of the body, either on or just in front of the backbone. However, they are linked with, and take their names from, locations on the front of the body, such as the navel, heart, throat and brow. They are generally reached in healing through the front of the body, though the root, or base, chakra is usually healed at the base of the spine or through the feet, where the energy makes contact with the Earth.

The chakras link with each other and with the areas of the body they control through *nadis,* thousands of tiny psychic energy lines. There are three main symbolic energy channels: the *sushumna,* a central channel that begins at the base of the spine and rises to an area at the base of the brain, and the *ida* and *pingala,* which extend from the base of the spine to the brow and end at the left and right nostrils. They criss-cross the sushumna in a twisted spiral like the entwined snakes of Mercury's staff, known as the caduceus.

The universal life force filters down via these channels to the chakras, each of which transforms the energy into the appropriate form for the function it governs.

Chakra energy itself is said to derive from a psychic Earth energy (the female power), called *kundalini-shakti* in Hindu Tantra, and *tumo* in Tibetan Buddhist Tantra. The kundalini energy is described as a coiled snake sleeping at the base of the spine until activated. It is identified with the female energy of Shakti, a name given to consorts of the Hindu Father God. The mingling and transference of all the energies creates a state of mental, physical, emotional and spiritual well-being.

Because these are psychic rather than actual physical centres, there is much debate over their precise location. This is further confused by the occasional overlap of names in different traditions. For example, I have always followed the theory that locates the solar plexus chakra, which controls will-power and digestion, just above the navel. But other writers and researchers locate it slightly higher, between the navel and the chest and, in fact, this chakra's influence seems to radiate over the whole area suggested by both traditions. For this reason, I am convinced that every one of us has a unique pattern of energies that can be traced with a pendulum or crystal. When healing others using these energy points, it is therefore important to trace not only the chakra locations but also the channels that join them. You will find that their paths will be specific to the individual, though following a general pattern.

Crystals and chakras

As we have already observed, crystals themselves radiate psychic energies and so they are especially effective for chakra work. They can, simply by being held close to a chakra point, release blockages and cleanse and empower the entire system. The more you use your crystals for personal chakra healing, the more they become attuned to your own bodily and spiritual rhythms, positively influencing your moods and energy flows. With this in mind, some people prefer to keep a special set of seven chakra crystals in a small bag for their personal use, with a few sprigs of fresh rosemary or sage that can be replaced at regular intervals to keep the life force flowing.

Each chakra, or energy centre, is linked with particular crystals or colours that can balance deficiencies or clear blockages in the physical and psychic body, and each chakra is also linked to a particular area of the body and mind. When the chakras are balanced and healthy, their colours are clear and luminous and they rotate smoothly. These colours can be seen clairvoyantly either in the auric field or sometimes as glowing centres within the body. When there is some physical imbalance or illness, pain or tension may be felt only in one place or not at all. However, the psychic energy centres reflect a wider view of the state of health, and so can show the source of the trouble, sometimes even before it is manifest on a physical level, offering a 'fast track' to healing. So the chakras are like an early warning system, and crystal healing of chakras that are blocked can stop problems before they have even started to develop fully.

The seven major chakras

As I have said, opinions differ as to the actual number and location of the chakras. However, it is generally accepted that there are seven main ones, and it is on these that I concentrate in this book.

The root chakra, or maladhara
Colour: Red

The root, or base, chakra is associated with physical functioning, basic instincts and the five physical senses. Physical pain and discomfort are manifest at this level. Pain and fever appear as a murky red in the afflicted area of the body or at the source of the infection, or will be reflected in the aura (see page 115 for reading the aura).

This chakra is rooted at the base of the spine, around the perineum, seat of the kundalini or basic energy source. It is linked with the legs, feet, skeleton and large intestine.

The root chakra uses red, raw energy to overcome fearsome odds and offers courage to make any necessary changes in your life.

Blockages can be reflected in problems with legs, feet and bones, and in bowel discomfort. On a psychological level, unreasonable anger at trivial causes can be a symptom of malfunction.

The sacral chakra, or svadisthana

Colour: Orange

This chakra is associated with spontaneous feelings and urges rather than consciously directed emotions; it is also linked to self-esteem and the emerging self-identity.

Though seated in the reproductive system, and so linked with fertility, it focuses on aspects of comfort or satisfaction, such as eating, drinking and sexuality. It controls the blood, reproductive system, kidneys, circulation and bladder.

The sacral chakra is the sphere of desire, the chakra of sensual pleasure and happiness.

Blockages can be reflected in problems with the reproductive system, bladder and circulatory system.

On a psychological level, problems will result in irritability and disorders involving physical indulgence.

The solar plexus chakra, or manipura

Colour: Yellow

This chakra is associated with the conscious mind, logic and mental power and control. It is seated around the navel, although some traditions place it slightly higher, between the navel and the chest. It controls digestion, the liver, spleen, stomach and small intestine.

The solar plexus chakra is the chakra of personal power, will and independence. This is the energy centre of digesting experiences, taking what is of use from life and casting aside what is redundant, so creating our sense of integrity and uniqueness.

Blockages in this area may be reflected in ulcers, indigestion, yellowy skin, feelings of nausea, and liver, gall-bladder, spleen and stomach problems. Eating disorders, where the balance of eating is upset and food necessary for strength and growth becomes attached to an emotional trigger (anorexia and bulimia are typical examples), also have their seat here.

On a psychological level, malfunction can lead to obsessions and over-concern for trivial detail.

The heart chakra, or anahata
Colour: Green

This chakra is associated with relationships and with emotional stability and harmony within the self as well as with others. It is situated in the centre of the chest, with its energies radiating over heart, lungs, breasts, arms and hands.

The heart chakra is the centre of altruism, compassion, unconditional love, sympathy and connection with both people and the environment, especially the natural world. Healing powers emanate from this chakra, especially when natural points of focus such as crystals and herbs are used. Blockages can be reflected in heart palpitations, hyperventilation, coughs and colds, lung problems and ailments in the hands and arms.

On a psychological level, free-floating anxiety or depression can stem from an imbalance in this area.

The throat chakra, or vishuddha

Colour: Blue

This chakra is associated with communication and idealism, the synthesis of emotion and thought. It is situated close to the Adam's apple in the centre of the neck. As well as the throat, speech organs and thyroid gland, the throat chakra controls the neck and shoulders and the passages that run up to the ears.

The throat chakra is the gateway between a personal and a more global perspective; it controls ideas, ideals, listening, speaking and giving creative form to thoughts.

Blockages may show themselves as frequent sore throats, colds, swollen glands and thyroid problems. They can also be reflected in problems with the neck, shoulders, speech organs, mouth, jaw, teeth and throat.

On a psychological level, confusion and incoherence result from an imbalance here.

The brow chakra, or savikalpa samadhi

Colours: Purple/indigo

This chakra, also known as the third eye, is associated with unconscious wisdom and psychic powers, especially clairvoyance but also clairaudience and mediumistic abilities.

It is situated just above the bridge of the nose in the centre of the brow and controls the eyes, ears and both hemispheres of the brain.

The brow chakra is the centre of inspiration and of awareness of a world beyond the material and immediate. At this level you may communicate with your higher self and your angelic and spirit guides and be able to see into past worlds. With the opening of this chakra, your healing powers take on a spiritual dimension, drawing on higher power. In your everyday life the power of this chakra is manifest as a highly sensitised intuitive awareness.

When this chakra is not functioning properly, you may experience a lot of headaches, earache, noises in your ears, eye infections or temporary blurring of vision that has no organic cause.

On a psychological level, insomnia or nightmares can result from malfunction.

The crown chakra, or nirvakelpa samadhi

Colour: Violet, seen as merging with white light pouring in from the cosmos

This chakra is associated with the merging of the spirit with the source of Divinity and with perfection in human terms.

The crown chakra is situated at the centre of the top of the head and rules the brain, body and psyche, as well as growth and well-being on physical, mental and spiritual levels. It is the centre of evolved creative and spiritual energy, the state in which mystical experiences occur, and represents pure spiritual awareness.

Blockages can be reflected in problems with the sinuses, skin and scalp, and general viruses and infections in the whole body that do not clear. You may feel tired but unable to relax, worried but unable to focus your actions on solutions.

On a psychological level, an inability to rise above everyday and material concerns, and a rigid attitude can result from a problem with this chakra.

Chakra crystals

Certain crystals correspond to particular chakras. It can be useful to have three or four of each chakra crystal (you need only buy small ones), as you can use softer shades for calming and the more vibrant ones for energising. You can also carry two or three as a talisman to empower you in particular situations ruled by that chakra.

The root chakra

Earthy red opaque stones such as red jasper or red tiger's eye, one of the banded red–brown agates, brown tiger's eye, black obsidian, iron pyrite (which when polished is a beautiful reddish-gold stone), bloodstone, garnet and ruby.

The sacral chakra

Orange glowing crystals such as carnelian, amber or rich opaque jasper, banded orange agate or orange sandstone pebbles; also rutilated quartz, haematite and moonstone.

The solar plexus chakra

For energising use sparkling citrine, topaz or yellow zircon; agates of any yellow or golden orange shade are especially good for balancing and stabilising energies. To soothe use gentler yellow crystals, fluorite or calcite.

The heart chakra

Pink and green stones of all kinds: green stones ranging from brilliant green malachite or deep green aventurine to softer jade, amazonite and moss agate; pink stones including bright rhodonite or rhosochrite, rose quartz and pink kunzite.

The throat chakra
Lapis lazuli and turquoise, for clearing physical and mental blockages; aquamarine and blue lace agate to relieve sore throats and painful glands and lessen the effects of a cold, and also to help aching tense shoulders or neck muscles.

The brow chakra
Amethyst, sodalite, sugilite and peacock's eye (bornite) – darker and more vibrant shades for psychic awareness and improved memory, paler hues to relieve headaches and anxiety.

The crown chakra
Clear quartz, brilliant purple sugilite, a rich deep violet and white banded amethyst or for gentler energies a cloudy quartz crystal.

Identifying and healing chakra imbalances

With crystals and a pendulum you can identify and heal all kinds of imbalances in the chakras. In the earlier sections on overall healing on pages 49–51 I have already described how you can use a crystal pendulum to identify channels of energy and remove any blockages. However, healing with specific chakra crystals can be helpful if there is a serious blockage or if there are a number of chakras that need attention.

Chakra healing with a pendulum

The method I describe here shows how this can be done, with the pendulum being used to identify problem areas and strengthen the flow of the life force after chakra healing.

* Pass your pendulum over your body, close to but not touching your skin. Move upwards, beginning from your left foot, and then downwards from the crown of your head to your right foot.

* Allow the pendulum to guide your path, but pause over the approximate sites of the seven main chakras and move the pendulum slowly clockwise until it taps into the swirl of the chakra – this will feel like a small psychic whirlpool. The pendulum may feel as though it is pulling down when it encounters the centre of power and may turn first backwards and then forwards over the power source. If the pendulum gradually falls into a gentle spiralling rhythm over the chakras, then the energies are flowing freely and need no intervention other than that supplied by the pendulum as it releases its innate gentle healing.

* If the pendulum seems sluggish or will move only anti-clockwise over a chakra, this may indicate a blockage. To clear this, move your pendulum in anti-clockwise circles while visualising the coloured light in the chakra becoming brighter as the darkness flows away.
* Once this is cleared, you can then energise the spot by moving the pendulum clockwise over the chakra and projecting light into the spot. There is usually rapid relief in an area of the body controlled by the chakra.

Chakra healing with crystals

If after using the pendulum you still encounter resistance or find that other chakras are similarly blocked, you can supplement your healing with specific chakra crystals before finally adding light through the pendulum. Begin with the lowest chakra where you find problems.

* Hold a chakra crystal in your power hand just over but not touching the affected chakra. Keep it entirely motionless at first, to establish the connection. You may experience a buzzing sensation in your fingers.
* Move the crystal clockwise in ever-increasing circles. As you do so, you can identify by the lessening of the connection the outer limits of the chakra. Just beyond these limits you may make connection with the energy field of one of the minor chakras or another major one, but you will feel a definite division, almost like a thin membrane. With experience, you will identify the separate energies by their slightly different energy patterns, which are manifest in subtly varying sensations.

* Starting from the centre of the chakra again, begin to move outwards in anti-clockwise circles and then inwards clockwise, very slowly and gently, stopping and holding the crystal still if there is a tangle of resistance. This will feel like a wheel in which string has caught and, as it untangles, so the 'wheel' will turn more easily.

* You can now energise the area additionally with clockwise movements of your pendulum to infuse it with the life force. Alternatively, you can wait until you have finished healing specific chakras and then energise the whole body. Remember to work from the left foot up to the crown, then down and out of the right foot.

You can use these methods for both yourself and other people. You can also carry out absent healing, using either the map method (see page 94) or a doll filled with healing herbs to identify the chakras of the absent person with a pendulum. You then apply chakra crystals to relevant areas of the figure.

Chakra crystal healing and the aura

I have already described how each of the colours of the aura is linked to a chakra. By interpreting the luminosity, dullness or even actual absence of a particular colour, you can identify any problems before they are manifest in actual symptoms and also heal the body, mind and spirit on such a deep and all-embracing level that well-being is restored.

Each chakra heart or centre contains a channel with a seal which when opened allows energy to pass from one auric level to another and ultimately into the physical body. Therefore when a particular auric colour appears to dominate the halo, you know that the corresponding chakra which creates that colour is providing the main energy input. This may be a good thing on a temporary basis but if you or the person you are healing always manifests one predominant colour, then the other chakras may need strengthening.

For example, when you are motivated by a fight-or-flight sensation as result of a confrontation, your root chakra energy will temporarily flood your aura with red. The effects will also be manifested physically: your skin may flush red and you may feel the adrenalin pumping. All this is temporary, however, and once the sensation has passed, the red colour and the other effects recede.

If, however, you dealt continually with emotional or relationship issues, major and minor, on this all-or-nothing level, the red would become a more permanent fixture in your aura. This would be because you were operating all the time through the root chakra, causing your aura and indeed your whole being to be out of balance.

How to read an aura in 60 seconds

Since the ability to read auras resides not in the physical but in the psychic eye, you have to learn to de-activate the conscious, analytical part of your mind and allow your unconscious wisdom to come through.

* Look at yourself in a mirror. If you are reading someone else's aura, get them to stand so that they are framed against light (some people prefer the subject with a darker background, so do experiment).

* Look at the area around the head, close your eyes for a few seconds, open them, blink and then you will get a vivid impression of the aura, either externally or in your mind's vision – both are equally good. It will appear like a rainbow, with the red colour closest to the body and the outermost violet layer extending up to an arm's span from the innermost layer.

* Record your impressions quickly in writing, diagrams, or however you wish. Your notes may say something like: 'Blue missing, red very harsh', and so on through the seven colours.
* Alternatively, until you trust this impression, draw seven concentric circles and take a set of coloured pencils in different shades. While looking at the aura, allow your hands to select the colours. This uses the same process as the pendulum, your hand guided by your unconscious mind. You can combine both methods, beginning by looking at the aura and then recording your impressions automatically. In both methods, you may record dark lines or streaks, jagged areas or even holes in the aura.

Interpreting and acting on your readings

As a general rule, a very pale shade or a missing colour needs extra crystal energy related to that chakra to be added. Harshness or jaggedness requires excess negativity to be removed by the appropriate chakra crystal. Dull, turgid colours indicate a blockage.

You can circle the relevant chakra location on your body anti-clockwise with its crystal to remove negativity and cleanse any blocked chakras.

Moving the crystal clockwise adds energy to a chakra. In both cases make slow, gentle movements until you can sense in the crystal a change in the energies, rather like a stream of flowing liquid crystal passing through your fingers.

The healing of the individual chakras will be reflected in clearer, brighter colours in the aura almost at once.

Chakra crystal balancing

As well as using crystals to heal and remove blockages in the chakras, you can also use them to maintain overall chakra balance and well-being. This can be carried out for other people, perhaps as part of other healing work or in a session after healing to ensure well-being is maintained.

It is a good idea to make a quiet time one evening each week when you will be undisturbed. Prepare yourself first. Turn off computers, mobile phones and telephones. Have a bath to which a few drops of lavender, rose or ylang ylang essential oil have been added. This will increase psychic awareness and mark the boundaries to the everyday world beyond which you pass in your crystal work. Light purple candles and sandalwood or frankincense incense sticks in a safe place.

* Lie on a bed or comfortable couch. Alternatively, you may like to carry this work out on a warm moonlit beach or in a sunlit meadow – it is wonderfully relaxing and you will need no artificial light or fragrance.

* You are now going to place a chakra crystal on each of the seven main chakras of your body. (It is slightly easier if someone else places the crystals, but quite possible to do it yourself if you begin at the feet and position the brow and crown chakra crystals when you are lying down.) Use flat rather than rounded crystals – if necessary you can use a little tape to secure them.

Root chakra: Place a dark red or brown crystal on the front of each ankle. The foot is the point where your body normally makes contact with the Earth, and the rich brown energy flows in and out of the coiled snake at the base of the spine and upwards.

Sacral chakra: Place an orange crystal on your womb or genitals.

Solar plexus chakra: Place a yellow crystal just above your navel.
Heart chakra: Place a green crystal in the centre of your chest or between your breasts, level with your heart.
Throat chakra: Place a blue crystal around the Adam's apple.
Brow chakra: Place a purple crystal on the centre of the brow just above the eyes.
Crown chakra: Place a clear quartz or white crystal on your hair line, in the centre.

* Close your eyes and allow the colours to swirl upwards and downwards, merging and forming rainbow light beams. Do not worry about visualising the energies. If you are working with someone else, play soft music and create a scene with words. Gaze at each crystal and words will come about crystal fountains, rainbows, flowing waters, warm sunlit grass, waterfalls and a gentle sea.

* When you have finished, look into the mirror and you will 'see' psychically that the area around your head appears quite luminous. Read the aura and note any areas that may need future care because the energy is still showing signs of depletion or over-activity at specific chakra points. Some imbalances take several treatments to put right.

* If there are any areas of discomfort or pain that you know need special attention, you can place three or four of the relevant chakra colours on the skin above the actual body part (see pages 105–9 for the areas ruled by each chakra). For a mental or spiritual difficulty you can circle the relevant chakra with crystals on the surface of the skin.

* Remember to wash your chakra crystals under running water and allow them to dry naturally.

Using chakra crystals in daily life

You may have an ongoing problem or need to strengthen one of your chakras for a particular purpose (for example, you may wish to boost your throat chakra if you have important communications to make). In this case, there are various ways to absorb the power of your crystals.

You can soak an appropriate chakra crystal in water (see pages 110–11) for 24 hours and drink the water, splash it on your pulse and the relevant chakra points or add it to your bath. Alternatively, you can add a chakra crystal or two to your bath water, or you can carry the relevant chakra crystals with you in a small purse or drawstring bag. You could either carry two or three relating to the problem chakra or one for each of the seven chakras for balance and well-being.

Empowering chakra crystals

You can empower your crystals to have both positive and protective qualities.

* Make a circle formation of the chosen chakra crystals.
* Surround them with a circle of salt, saying:

  I *charge you with the power of Earth. Protect, empower and inspire.*

* Light a frankincense or sandalwood incense stick and make a circle of smoke round the crystals, saying:

  I *charge you with the power of Air. Protect, empower and inspire.*

* Circle them with a white or beeswax candle, saying:

  I *charge you with the power of Fire. Protect, empower and inspire.*

* Make a circle of water in which an amethyst and clear crystal quartz have been soaked for 24 hours, saying:

I charge you with the power of Water. Protect, empower and inspire.

* Finally, circle them once more with your incense, saying:

Earth, Air, Water, Fire, protect, empower and inspire.

You can use this method for empowering any crystals. If you are stressed or feel that your energies are blocked, you can hold the relevant chakra crystal in your power hand and visualise the colours flowing. If in doubt, a root chakra crystal will give you protection against malice and strength to survive and a crown crystal will send instant energy and inspiration throughout the entire system very fast.

Chapter 8
Crystal Healing at Home and at Work

Many people who have never practised crystal healing or visited a healer nevertheless find that crystals release therapeutic powers in the home and workplace, reducing stress and protecting against negativity. Fluorescent lighting and the constant jangling of mobile phones, faxes, computers and machinery all make the workplace a tangle of noise and pollution. At home, too, televisions, stereos, freezers, microwaves and the frantic whirl of activity can wear down our natural immunity to illness. Moreover, some places do actually seem to have negative energies that emanate from the land.

Crystals can offer a valuable shield from all forms of negativity and assaults upon the senses and from the unremitting pressures that our pre-technological ancestors did not experience. This ongoing form of crystal healing can prevent stress escalating. There are a number of crystals that work especially well for workplace and home protection, and you can use them in many ways. For example, you could keep a large ornamental crystal on a table, desk or workbench, wear a crystal pendant, earrings or cufflinks or have a special lucky or soothing crystal in a pocket or pouch. You can place a dish of smaller crystals on a table at home or in your workspace and hold one as you talk on the telephone or whenever you are involved in a potentially stressful interaction. This will deflect any pressures that may come your way. When faced with difficult friends, relatives or colleagues, you can make coffee or tea or serve mineral water in which a healing crystal bringing gentleness has been soaked. You can add crystals directly to your bath water – energising ones in the morning and after work, soothing ones to melt away the tensions of the day.

Crystals in the workplace

If you do keep crystals in the workplace over a period of months, you will gradually detect an improvement in the atmosphere. There may be fewer confrontations, at least in your own area, and you yourself will be less affected by stress and so not only perform better but come home less tired and able to relax more easily. You may find that you start a trend. Giving crystals as presents to colleagues pays dividends in the positivity that is generated by the crystalline energies.

To deflect stress from constant interruptions that may not be unfriendly but eat into your time, place a large gentle protective crystal with a pointed end in your personal work space. Rose quartz or amethyst are good choices. Keep the point facing a wall under normal circumstances, but when an unwelcome intrusion comes your way, turn the crystal round so the point will repel the unwanted visitor. Because the crystal is gentle, it will not cause harm; it will merely act as a barrier. You will see that the person will stop, maybe look puzzled, as if trying to remember why he or she was heading your way and then be diverted to another location.

If there is genuine hostility, backbiting or destructive gossip that you wish to avoid, use a citrine or clear crystal quartz to reflect the light. A rounded one will work well and will surround you in a golden or pure white shield if you breathe in the light and cast it all around you. It reflects back any potential threat on to the sender. This may not sound like the province of healing, but the negative karma of others is not relieved by their being unpleasant to you and certainly will not improve your well-being. Mirrors are also often used for the same purpose.

You can even use crystals for temporary invisibility by keeping smoky quartz in your drawer or on your work bench. You will not actually disappear, of course, but your profile may be lowered – useful when you are trying to meet a deadline and do not want interruptions. When you see distraction heading your way, open the drawer, breathe in the dark light around you and exhale brightness. When the potential interruption has passed, splash clear crystal quartz water on your face and wrists to restore the energy. This also works well if you find yourself unavoidably in a dangerous place at night.

If you are involved in a phone call that unexpectedly becomes confrontational or destructive, to absorb negativity circle a rose quartz or amethyst anti-clockwise around the phone as you speak. You can do the same around your computer if unfriendly e-mails arrive.

Circling your computer each morning with green and black malachite helps to protect against computer viruses, but don't forget to update your conventional virus programme regularly as well.

Bury tiny moss agate crystals in the soil of workplace plants to relieve their stress and the effects on them of central heating.

When you have used protective crystals, hold them under running water as soon as possible.

Reducing stress at home

There are two kinds of domestic negativity that benefit from continuous crystal healing: bad vibes that enter the home from outside pressures and internal quarrels or tensions.

To deflect unwanted pressures from outside, place a dark crystal on either side of your doorways, front and back. Best are the earthing agates, jet or a dark jasper to balance and strengthen the boundaries. You can also bury small agates at the corners of your boundaries and on each side of gates.

Inside, each room should have crystals to harmonise the energies. So in a dining room, keep carnelian and amber to stimulate appetite and overcome food fads, citrine to aid digestion and encourage positive interactions, and blue lace agate for gentleness in words to avoid confrontations or careless speech. The bedrooms will benefit from rose quartz, amethyst and moonstones for quiet sleep and happy dreams.

In the main sitting areas, create a crystalline water feature with a pot, a small electric pump, some water plants, and jade, turquoise and aquamarine crystals to wash away tensions and promote harmony and loving relationships.

In any work areas, such as a study or home office, clear crystal quartz for creativity might be balanced by deep blue sodalite or lapis lazuli for connection with higher energies and for preventing workaholics from beavering the night away.

The kitchen needs warm stimulating crystals, such as blood agates and red jasper, balanced by malachite and also jade to counter the effects of electrical goods and to prevent fires or accidents.

The bathroom should, obviously, contain the sea crystal aquamarine, and there should be a dish of different crystals to add to bath water: clear crystal quartz for energy, turquoise for inspiration, jade for gentle restorative energies after a hard day, citrine for optimism and focus, rose quartz for healing and soothing, amethysts to slow down hyperactivity and obsessive thoughts, and agates for balancing. When bathing, if you are not certain of the energies you need, close your eyes and reach into the dish, allowing your unconscious mind to make the connection. You may be surprised to find you have selected a relaxing crystal when you thought you were quite calm. However, selection by this method is invariably accurate.

Remember to keep a good supply of crystalline waters for different purposes ready in the fridge.

Negative Earth energies

Sometimes, however, no matter what you do, a workplace or house can feel unfriendly and you can have a series of minor illnesses or a run of bad luck that are shared by colleagues even though there is no obvious cause. Irritability, quarrels that spring from nowhere and a feeling that a room is always cold or dark even in bright sunlight may indicate that the building is constructed on a site where there are strong negative Earth energies. Many people believe that lines of psychic energy, called ley lines, run under the Earth and that where they cross, a sudden surge of energy not conducive to mundane living can be generated. Certainly, the Earth itself is a seething mass of activity deep below the surface (witness volcanic action or an earthquake and you will be in no doubt of its power), and all kinds of magnetic and radioactive rays have been measured at different places. We also know that animals and even plants do not thrive in certain places. Cats will not sit in an apparently comfortable spot and plants will wilt even though light and heat conditions are apparently optimum. Such spots are said to be sites of negative Earth energies.

Neutralising negative Earth energies

Whatever the cause of negative energies, it is not always possible to move yourself to a different location. However, crystals can both detect and remedy this negativity.

If you sense that something is not quite right about your home or workplace, walk around the area with your crystal pendulum and ask it to indicate any places where there are problems. The pendulum may feel heavy or swing in an anti-clockwise circle. You can specifically direct your pendulum by saying: 'Show me by your negative response if there are negative Earth energies here that may be detrimental to health and well-being.'

Plot on a chart of your home or workplace, each place where you experience the negative swing of the pendulum. Once you have located these places, you can effectively neutralise them with crystals.

Amethyst crystals are perhaps the most effective stones for neutralising all forms of negative Earth energies. Small amethyst inclusions still in the rock are not expensive and make excellent paperweights or ornaments. Rose quartz too will take away any jagged edges of harsh energy. Position these crystals near the centre of the spot of negative energy, on small tables.

Tiny amethyst crystals can be placed under the carpet or behind work equipment, and you can create a crystal trail following the lines or patterns of the negative spots.

Check with your pendulum and if you still have problems add a smoky quartz or obsidian to soak up the negativity.

Recharge your crystals once a week, or more frequently if you sense the darker energies seeping back.

Using your crystal pendulum, you may find where the darker energies enter a building. If so, block this with stones containing quartz found on a sea shore or near a river.

Protective crystals for home and workplace

Aquamarine

Colours: Clear light blue, blue-green to dark blue

This is a stone associated with the sea and with water. It is protective for all journeys, especially by sea. As a water stone it calms stress and comforts those who are grieving or in extreme mental or spiritual pain. It also fosters tolerance in situations that cannot be changed.

Aquamarine encourages clear communication, creativity and confidence.

If the crystal is placed overnight in water which is drunk first thing in the morning, the drink is said to cleanse the whole body. Place aquamarines in your bath water to induce tranquillity.

Bloodstone (heliotrope)

Colours: Opaque, mottled green and red

In Ancient Babylon bloodstone was used in amulets for protection against enemies. Bloodstone is primarily a stone of courage and was carried by soldiers in many cultures to overcome fears and to protect against wounding. Therefore this is a stone to carry if you fear enemies of any kind or face spite or malice. It also repels psychic attack.

Desert rose

Colours: Light brown, opaque with glints

Although this rough textured stone is not immediately attractive, resembling a walnut rather than a crystal, desert rose is the stone of all who wander far from home or seek inner understanding. Desert rose contains an inner store of wisdom; an earthing stone, it reduces anxiety and calms racing thoughts.

Garnet

Colours: Shining dark red, also green, orange and colourless

Primarily a protective stone. Eastern European peoples used the garnet against illness, night phantoms and all forms of evil, including the mythical vampire. In mediaeval times, garnets were engraved with a lion's head for health and safe travel, and the garnet is still regarded as a stone for travellers, especially against attack. Like the emerald, it is said to change colour if danger is near.

Garnets also provide energy when rest is not possible.

Haematite

Colour: Silver-grey, metallic, brilliant

A powerful earthing and protective stone that activates natural survival instincts. The Ancient Egyptians used it to soothe hysteria and worries. Strongly linked to the physical body, haematite acts as a shield against potential physical and emotional hostility.

Jet

Colour: Black

Jet is fossilised wood that has been turned into a dense form of coal and is a very protective stone against sorrow and all forms of negativity. It has been used from early times as an amulet.

Jet will guard travellers and fishermen from all harm. Traditionally the wives of sailors would keep a jet amulet at home so that their husbands would return safely from the sea. Jet prevents nightmares and is said to help the user to face the ending of a natural phase so that they can move on to the next.

Lapis lazuli

Colours: Opaque rich medium to dark blue with flecks of iron pyrite (fool's gold)

Known as the eye of wisdom and the stone of the gods, lapis lazuli in jewellery has for thousands of years been credited with healing and protective powers. The Sumerians believed it contained the souls of their gods and goddesses and as such would endow them with magical powers and the protection of the deities themselves.

In Egypt, lapis lazuli was first used in a powdered form for eye make-up and women would circle their eyes with the powder as protection against the evil eye. This is a stone that has retained its reputation for protection against malevolence from spirit as well as earthly sources.

Malachite

Colour: Opaque green with black stripes

A purifier and energiser, malachite replaces negativity, anger and depression with positive energies and physical and emotional pain with warmth and a sense of well-being; it cleanses the auric field, and is also effective for absorbing pollution and the enervating energies from computers, faxes, mobile phones and televisions. Because it works so hard, malachite should be cleansed at least every two days.

Obsidian (Apache tears)
Colours: Translucent black to dark smoky grey

Obsidian absorbs dark energies and converts them to white healing light; hold your obsidian up to the light and see better days ahead.

Powerful for earthing, obsidian is an antidote to illusion and escapism. It absorbs and dissolves anger, protects sensitive people from unfair criticism and helps users to release regrets for lost love or happiness; another stone for travellers.

Sodalite
Colours: Deep blue or purple, often with white flecks, white and indigo

Sodalite alleviates subconscious guilt and fears and offers protection from negative energies of all kinds. Placed next to computers, fax machines, etc., sodalite is believed to reduce the effects of the harmful rays that emanate from such technological and electrical equipment.

Topaz
Colours: Clear, sparkling, golden, champagne-coloured, pink, pale blue, orange or brown

The name means 'fire' in Sanskrit. Topaz increases in power with the Moon, being at its greatest potency at the time of the full Moon. Perhaps because of this, topaz is said to be proof against supernatural creatures of the night, nightmares and night terrors.

Water in which a topaz has been soaked is a cure for insomnia if drunk an hour before bedtime. According to ancient Eastern belief, topaz confers invisibility on its wearer and so is good for lowering one's profile in potentially hazardous or confrontational situations. It is especially good for defusing violent emotions whether in self or others. Golden topaz is excellent for alleviating work anxieties and so should be kept in the workplace.

Chapter 9
Crystal Healing for Children and Animals

In the Introduction, I spoke about the natural ability that children have to heal with crystals. They are also very open to crystalline healing energies and so are ideal patients with whom you can gain confidence as you develop your own healing powers. Because children are so psychically aware, they merge easily with crystals. You can give them a bag of crystals of their own with which they can play, weave stories, heal first their dolls and teddy bears, and then pets and humans. However, you must be sure that they are old enough to use them without the risk of swallowing them or hurting themselves by dropping a heavy sphere.

Young children will instinctively place amethyst on their head and jade on their heart and hold clear quartz in their hand while making wishes. If you feel unwell, ask a child to choose you a crystal that will make you feel better.

Watch their techniques as they work, the easy unselfconscious strokes with the crystal and the gentle pressure that seems to melt away tension or pain. If a child offers to make your headache better, accept the offer. You will not deplete their strength, for they are plugged into the life force, nor do they need psychic protection for healing work. Their innate innocence and goodness attracts angelic guides all around them (but see pages 138–40 for crystals that will drive away their fears).

Crystal gifts

A crystal can be a lovely gift for a newborn baby, perhaps given at a naming ceremony or when you first visit a newborn. For your own children you might like to buy a crystal when you first feel the baby kicking inside. If your children are older, crystals are a perfect birthday or special occasion gift. You could also take a child to a museum shop or a mineral store and allow him or her to select small crystals. There will be none of the hesitation of the adult. After initially touching the different trays of stones (choose a child-friendly place where the experience will be pleasurable), their choice will be almost instant.

For a special crystal, you might choose a birthstone (see Chapter 10 for zodiacal significances). Alternatively, you could place all your own healing crystals in a drawstring bag, focus on the child, born or unborn, and allow your unconscious wisdom to select a stone that links with the psyche of the infant. I find this even more accurate than relying on conventional zodiacal correlations for children and adolescents. If the child is unborn at the time of selection, you will often find that he or she grows up matching the qualities of the stone you chose – the rose quartz peacemaker and gentle spirit or the quicksilver carnelian, a noble lion even at five or six years of age.

You can add a crystal to your child's collection for each birthday. Each significant step – starting or changing school, moving house, additions to the family or a loss, an important examination – can be marked by a crystal gift that offers strength or reassurance at a time of change (I give more suggestions for these in Chapter 11).

Wash crystals in running water before giving them as gifts, and hold each up to the light of the Sun or full Moon, endowing it with wishes for the child's future health and happiness.

Crystals for a baby can be dangled near the cradle to catch the light, or for small children suspended in a silver cradle affixed to a chain at the bedroom window. These you can buy from any jeweller's or mineral store, or you can make your own, weaving wires of gold for the Sun, silver for the Moon and copper for Venus, who rules all love and gentle growth.

Even a child of two or three can play with crystals under supervision. Instead of a bedtime story, you can allow him or her to choose a crystal from your bag and tell them the story of the crystal angel or fairy, of the beautiful Princess Jade or the magical tiger who lives within amber. Then place the crystal in a safe place next to the child's own protective crystal (see pages 136 and 137–40) to ensure quiet sleep and peaceful dreams.

Healing with special crystals

In time, one crystal may acquire especially strong healing powers for the child's illnesses. Often it is the birth crystal or perhaps one given or chosen at a particularly significant time. When a child's illness is acute or prolonged then, of course, we would seek conventional medical help. But as parents we do have an instinctive knowledge of when time and sleep are the best healers, and there is also an increasing awareness that over-use of antibiotics for relatively minor ills will create problems of its own.

So if a child complains of a head or ear pain or a sore throat, you can try dipping an amethyst in water and applying it to the brow or gently warming a rose quartz and pressing it to the ear. So too for a minor sore throat you can encourage the child to drink or gargle with blue lace agate water. Small children love helping to make coloured crystal waters. You may wish to follow up crystal healing with a honey and lemon drink or gentle analgesic.

Even if you do need to consult a doctor, crystals can still heal and soothe, helping to trigger the natural immune system. Many mothers with teething babies create an amulet of coral or jade to hang over the sleeping area. In earlier times, teething rings were made of coral, and small children wore coral necklaces or bracelets to protect them when falling over. Older children may carry their crystal in a pocket or pouch to help them at school, especially to guard against teasing and as a luck-bringer and focus for memory in examinations.

If a child loses their special crystal, don't despair. Buy one as similar as you can and soak it in water in which there are rose petals, with the child visualising all the powers from the old crystal flowing into the new. Picture the lost crystal in an ideal setting, in the bed of a river, or on a sandy seashore. Then go with the child out of doors as it is getting dark, and when you both see the first star, follow the age-old tradition of holding up the crystal and saying:

> *Starlight, star bright,*
> *First star I see tonight.*
> *I wish I may, I wish I might*
> *Have the wish I make tonight.*

However, instead of making a wish, transfer the wish power into the crystal. This can also be effective in giving a crystal additional potency if a child is really worried about a situation or event. Of course, you could always let the child dowse for the lost crystal with a pendulum, using a map of the location. As with all psychic arts, children are instinctively expert dowsers.

Protection for children

All children, especially sensitive ones, suffer fears, nightmares and night terrors. A traumatic situation at home or school can lead to insomnia, nervous tics or general irritability. Once you have tackled the root cause of the problem, a specially empowered protective crystal can act as a talisman against harm. Allow your child to choose a crystal that they feel offers protection; often this is a dark stone, such as a smoky quartz that when you hold it to the Sun reveals light and hope, but they may choose a Sun stone, such as citrine, or a carnelian lion of courage stone.

After dusk, light a ring of small deep purple crystals with the special crystal in the centre. Sit with the child at a safe distance and together breathe in the purple light and breathe out darkness, picturing the light extending all around the crystal and the child in a purple sphere. Tell the child that this is a ring of protection and whenever he or she feels sad or afraid, just by touching, holding or even visualising the crystal, the purple shield of protection can be activated.

If the child is being bullied or threatened, use golden candles and visualise sparks radiating from the golden sphere to repel harm.

Should a child or teenager be especially anxious, put a plug in the sink or washbasin when you wash the crystal under running water. The child can put the crystal in the water and swirl it nine times anti-clockwise, saying: 'Sorrow cease, go in peace.'

Then he or she can remove the crystal and pull out the plug, watching the water flow away and saying: 'Flow, go, far from me, from the rivers to the sea.'

Healing children

The following crystals are, in my own experience, especially good for children:

Amethyst

This stone, which ranges from pale lilac to deep purple and white, soothes nightmares and in its darker shades of purple is very protective. It is especially good for calming anxieties, relieving nervous habits and for soothing pain, especially if tension-related.

Carnelian

This translucent orange or red stone inspires courage. In Roman times it was engraved with the head of a lion or a great leader to drive away all fears and can balance the gentler emotions of sensitive children and teenagers. Carnelian enhances self-esteem and self-confidence and so is good for new situations, for times of change or if a child or teenager is self-conscious about their appearance.

Coral

This organic gem comes in many shades of pink, red and even orange. Particularly associated with babies and young children, it is very protective against all kinds of harm in the young, guarding against spite, bullying and sarcasm, especially from insensitive adults. Coral is warming for tooth and ear pains or swollen glands.

Jade

Jade is a gentle healer and is a wonderful stone for balancing hormonal swings and unstable emotions during the teenage years. Another stone that promotes self-love, jade, like rose quartz, is helpful if there is family conflict and at times of change. Chinese children often have jade amulets, and the stone encourages a harmonious path to independence, allaying fears and relieving a sense of loneliness. Jade is good for growing pains and to prevent coughs, colds and virus infections.

Rose quartz
This pink transparent crystal is another valuable stone for children and teenagers and, with amethyst, is usually the first stone they spontaneously select for healing. It is deeply protective against sorrow and cruelty and will heal negative experiences. Many adults with unresolved childhood sorrow or abuse find this stone very helpful. Reassuring for children and teenagers who are away from home, rose quartz also relieves rashes, head and ear pains, muscle pains and hyperactivity. A stone of the heart, it is a powerful transmitter of gentle affection within the family and in times of family uncertainty.

Smoky quartz
Not an obvious stone for children, this semi-transparent brown, grey or black crystal is nevertheless often selected as an amulet. As I said earlier, when it is held to the Sun or a candle flame, light shines through it, promising better days ahead. With its gradual release of energies it also contains the power to help a child or teenager fight back against difficulties. Smoky quartz is good for driving away fears of the dark and for protecting the child from dangerous situations and strangers.

Tiger's eye

This golden brown translucent stone exudes courage and was carried by soldiers in Rome to prevent panic. It is also deeply empowering and can be used to create a psychic shield of gold (see page 137). Tiger's eye will attract success to the young person, especially in mid-teenage years. Above all it will help to bring pride in his or her achievements as well as focus. It endows the child and teenager with the power to resist temptation from unwise friends and stabilise impulsive behaviour. It helps allergies and stress conditions.

Crystals and animals

Your pets, like your children, are good subjects for crystal healing because there is a bond of love between owner and animal, providing a psychic channel along which the healing energies can flow.

Crystals can be used to maintain the health and well-being of your pets. Some owners regularly give their pets water in which jade has been soaked to bring them long life and health. Amber is a gentle energiser and is not as fierce as clear quartz or citrine, which can be too intense for an animal. Keeping jade or moss agate under the corners of a pet bed or securing a single crystal in a bird cage will infuse gradual health-enhancing qualities and calm a hyperactive or nervous animal.

If you take in from a rescue centre an animal who perhaps has been neglected or ill-treated, a mixture of rose quartz and jade will diminish bad memories and restore trust.

If the animal is happy for you to do so, once or twice a week very gently massage its fur with jade in clockwise circles to energise the innate life force. However, if your pet is reluctant to be touched directly with a crystal – often because it is extra sensitive to healing powers – make clockwise circles a short distance away from the fur or feathers, following the aura or psychic energy field that surrounds the animal. In a dog, cat or horse, this is often seen either in the mind's vision or externally as a rich brown or soft pink or green haze. Birds are surrounded by shades of blue, grey and silver. Stop healing when the pet becomes restless.

Earth stones, such as brown and banded agates, golden brown rutilated quartz and jaspers, tend to work best to reconnect a sick animal to the healing flow from the Earth. Quartz pebbles you find on the sea shore, which appear quite dull until you hold them to the light, add the healing of the waters to their Earth power and so are especially good to circle around fish tanks.

However, it is a sky stone, turquoise, that for thousands of years has been particularly associated with the healing and protection of animals. Turquoise is plaited into the mane of a horse or attached to the bridle to prevent it stumbling. It can also be fixed to pets' collars and to the mirrors of caged birds to prevent theft or loss.

If an animal is unwell or in pain it may not appreciate being touched with a crystal, though some enjoy gentle stroking well away from the site of the discomfort or wound.

Work in natural light, in the early morning or just before dusk, and begin with a single Earth crystal (see next page for suggestions). Try to connect with the animal's breathing as it sleeps or rests. You are acting as a direct transmitter for the Earth light, breathing in the crystal energy slowly and regularly and exhaling the rich brown or golden light in the direction of the animal, where it will flow round and enter the auric field. Merge not with the crystal but the animal, becoming its slow breathing, scenting the Earth, the bushes low down, the tiny scurrying creatures, and see your pet as well and whole again. Continue until you feel the channels fading. At this point the animal has received sufficient healing and you should sit quietly sending love. The pet may stir in its sleep, grunt or sigh with relief.

Wash the crystal under running water and store it with fresh leaves of a healing herb such as sage, rosemary or thyme or with small branches of cedar, ash, olive or aspen – these are healing trees.

Keep gentle healing stones, such as rutilated quartz, banded agates or fossilised wood, under the four corners of your pet's bed during the illness and convalescence, and renew these regularly by placing them in a pot of healing herbs such as lavender or chamomile for 48 hours. This is a good method for cleansing any crystals used in animal work.

A drink of water in which amethyst or rose quartz has been soaked for 24 hours will restore your pet's depleted energies.

Using crystals with very sick or old animals

Sometimes asking for recovery from an illness may not be the kindest thing and what we really want is a gentle passing for our beloved animal. When my old cat Haegl became very ill, she actually welcomed death, and animals in the wild will often seek a quiet, private place to die.

Very dark Earth crystals, deep banded agates, dark brown jasper, fossilised wood and the darker shades of smoky quartz or obsidian will ease the passing.

Make a soft dark private place for your pet to lie – your animal may find one itself. Ring this at a distance with dark Earth crystals.

Using deep amethyst, breathe in the light through your nose and cast a violet shield around the creature as you exhale. Do not try to merge with the animal but visualise a crystal guardian within the sphere holding and comforting your animal. The crystal may seem deeper in colour as you work and, by the time the animal dies, it may appear quite luminous as the guardian powers increase.

Work for no more than three or four minutes at a time and then very softly, at a slight distance, speak soothing words expressing your love and gratitude for your time together.

Repeat the colour breathing two or three times a day, working in gentle natural light or growing darkness. You will see that the purple sphere around the animal grows larger and if you are working over a period of days that the purple light forms a gentle halo even before you begin healing.

When the animal dies, the light will be gone and the crystal will return to its normal colour. However, you may sense that your animal is well and strong again or even feel its soft fur brush against you. I have received so many accounts of animal ghosts that I have no doubt that animals' spirits do survive death. I have also been sent a number of stories of pets that died at the same time as their owners.

Bury the crystals with your animal.

Crystals for healing animals

Agates

Colours: Opaque, red, orange, yellow, brown, black, banded and single colour

These beautiful Earth rainbows occur in muted shades that blend with one another and are excellent for the gentle healing of all ills in pets. Use the darker colours for chronic or terminal illness or when a pet is very old. They balance the animals' energies and link them with the power of the Earth. They also protect the animal from the stress of noise, especially in towns.

Obsidian (Apache tears)

Colour: Black

These can be good crystals with which to calm animals if they are due to go for an operation or even to visit the vet (which most pets hate), as obsidians allay fears and induce acceptance of what cannot be changed.

Older animals can benefit from this gentle protective power over a period of months even when they are quite well, as it will encourage them to rest sufficiently. If an animal has experienced a bad fright or suffered abuse for a prolonged period from a previous owner or while straying, obsidian under the pet bed will erase bad memories.

Jade

Colours: All shades of green, opaque to transparent

A natural transmitter of life energies, jade encourages longevity in animals. Use the softer opaque shades when energising water. You can also clean food bowls in a similar manner, especially for newly weaned animals or those that are delicate.

You might like to buy a set of jade crystals when you first obtain your pet. They will be enhanced by the unique energies of the creature and you can use them in rotation. Jade is very helpful for an animal giving birth. My black cat Jenny insisted I stay with her while she had her litter, and I ringed the basket she chose for delivery with jade and breathed green light upon her.

Jasper

Colours: Opaque, multi-coloured, single colours, yellow, orange, brown, green, also sometimes found as petrified wood

Jasper is another crystal associated with nature. In its gentler colours – brown, green and orange – it is a stone that brings strength as it heals and can boost the immune system. It is a good stone for healing animals approaching maturity. Should you have a pet snake, the mottled leopardskin jasper, sometimes called snakeskin jasper, should be placed in the tank when it is shedding its skin. It also helps other creatures through transitions, for example a house move or the arrival of new members of the family. Black, like brown, jasper will aid a very sick or dying animal to move on.

Place jasper near bird tables to encourage and protect wild birds.

Rutilated quartz

Colours: Clear quartz with metallic golden rutile, copper, or blue-grey titanium fibres

Rutilated quartz will amplify other crystal healing and speed recovery. It is especially good for older animals as it can encourage gentle qualities in a bad-tempered or snappy animal. Because of this, it is also good when training younger animals or breaking destructive habits in older ones who have been unkindly treated.

Turquoise

Colours: Opaque, light blue, blue-green

Mined by the Egyptians in Sinai more than 6,000 years ago, turquoise is especially protective of horses. A turquoise on a collar or in a cage will guard any animal against theft or harm. Turquoise absorbs negativity and pollutants so is good for creatures who live in towns, especially those exposed to traffic fumes. It is very soothing for restless animals and birds, and nevertheless enables the animal to retain its unique personality. Use it to heal sudden or acute conditions and to prevent accidents as well as to protect against the malevolence of animal-haters.

Chapter 10
Healing with Zodiacal Crystals

The belief in the magical power of crystals dates back thousands of years. As early as the time of the Chaldeans, who lived in Mesopotamia in 4000 BC and studied the stars for divinatory purposes, certain planets were linked to crystals that were said to reflect their energies and characteristics. In the sixteenth century, Francis Bacon remarked: 'So much is true ... that gems have fine spirits and may operate by consent on the spirits of men, to strengthen and exhilarate them.'

In the chapter on children (see page 134) I mentioned that a child could be given a special crystal at birth and that this need not be his or her birthstone. However, from my own work, I have discovered that adults seem to relate well to a birthstone both for healing and empowerment.

There is considerable disagreement over the precise stone or crystal linked with each zodiacal period, and this gives rise to some doubt as to their validity. These discrepancies arise because over thousands of years and in different cultures, the month stones, as they were formerly called (zodiacal birthstones as such were not introduced until the early eighteenth century), varied in different parts of the world and in different spiritual practices and religions.

Some of these stones have remained consistent across cultures. For example, the February (now Aquarius) crystal is the amethyst in almost every tradition. Pisceans born in the last half of February also have a claim to amethyst as their birth stone. In contrast, the gems and crystals for the month of May have included agate, emerald, chalcedony, carnelian and more recently rose quartz.

The list I give combines several of the traditions where there is agreement, and is one I have adapted over the years as my own research into the subject has increased. While your stone is most potent for you on your birthday and during your personal Sun sign period, you can also use it at any other time you need strength, protection or healing.

Because there is a choice of stones, you can use the one that feels right for you. As you carry or wear it, so it will tune into your unique energy patterns and adapt its own energies so that it becomes a repository of healing powers for you. Other crystals of the same kind will be potent but your special stone will accumulate extra healing potency. You can carry or wear the relevant crystal and sleep with it under your pillow or near your bed. It will act as an amulet when you travel.

To absorb the energies of your stone, soak your birth crystal in water for 24 hours and drink the water or add the water to your bath. Gems are more delicate and so this method is not suitable for them, but their energies are transferable just by holding or wearing them.

To empower and cleanse your birth gem or crystal, once a week after dark pass it nine times anti-clockwise over a candle in your zodiacal colour, high above the flame so you do not burn yourself. This will cleanse it of any negativity it has acquired. Then pass it nine times clockwise over the flame to empower it. The stone will then act as a charm of power and protection.

Your birth stone

In the list below, I give the dates and properties associated with each of the 12 birthstones. Astrological dates may vary by a day or two according to the year and the system used. If your birthday lies on the cusp, you can use the crystals of the sign that seems most relevant.

I have also given the angel, who according to traditional lore, watches over the healing of this period. Allow a picture of the angel to come to you – each of us perceives our personal angel in a unique way. He or she may appear in your mind's vision surrounded by the coloured light of your crystal as you cleanse and empower your stone, or you may see your angel within the stone if it is transparent. As you empower the stone, you can ask for the blessings of the healing angel of the crystal.

♈ Aries, the Ram (21 March–20 April)
Stones: Bloodstone for determination, also diamond
Candle colour: Red
Guardian angel: Malchediel
Incense: Dragon's blood

♉ Taurus, the Bull (21 April–21 May)
Stones: Rose quartz for patience, also emerald
Candle colour: Pink
Guardian angel: Ashmodiel
Incense: Rose

♊ Gemini, the Heavenly Twins (22 May–21 June)

Stones: Citrine for versatility, also sapphire
Candle colour: Pale grey or yellow
Guardian angel: Ambriel
Incense: Lavender

♋ Cancer, the Crab (22 June–22 July)

Stones: Moonstone for gentle love, also pearl
Candle colour: Silver
Guardian angel: Muriel
Incense: Jasmine

♌ Leo, the Lion (23 July–23 August)

Stones: Carnelian for courage, also topaz
Candle colour: Gold
Guardian angel: Verchiel
Incense: Frankincense

♍ Virgo, the Maiden (24 August–22 September)

Stones: Jade for harmony, also sapphire
Candle colour: Green
Guardian angel: Hamaliel
Incense: Thyme

♎ Libra, the Scales (23 September–23 October)

Stones: Lapis lazuli for wisdom, also opal
Candle colour: Light blue

Guardian angel: Zuriel
Incense: Vanilla

♏ Scorpio, the Scorpion (24 October–22 November)
Stones: Banded agate for unconscious awareness, also aquamarine
Candle colour: Burgundy
Guardian angel: Barakiel (also rules over Pisces)
Incense: Pine

♐ Sagittarius, the Archer (23 November–21 December)
Stones: Ruby for inner fire, also turquoise
Candle colour: Yellow
Guardian angel: Adnachiel
Incense: Sandalwood

♑ Capricorn, the Goat (22 December–20 January)
Stones: Garnet for fidelity, also ruby or jacinth
Candle colour: Indigo or brown
Guardian angel: Hamael
Incense: Cedar

♒ Aquarius, the Water Carrier (21 January–18 February)
Stones: Amethyst for integrity, also spinel
Candle colour: Dark blue
Guardian angel: Cambiel
Incense: Patchouli

♓ Pisces, the Fish (19 February–20 March)

Stones: Jasper for intuitive awareness, also beryl
Candle colour: White or mauve
Guardian angel: Barakiel
Incense: Honeysuckle

A self-healing ritual using your zodiacal crystal

You can work with this ritual to heal a specific illness or feeling of malaise or anxiety. Alternatively, you can use it as a personal affirmation whenever you need strength or protection or to increase your own healing powers for helping others. It can be a good prelude to absent healing if you are working alone, perhaps with your healing book, and especially if you lack energy yourself.

Wait until after dusk and make a circle of small candles of your birth colour. The circle should be large enough to sit in safely without burning yourself.

* Place a candle at each of the compass positions, north, south, east and west. I like to use eight candles, placing the extra four at the north-east, south-east, south-west and north-west compass positions. If you prefer, you can make the circle on a table and sit just beyond, visualising yourself within the circle of light.

* Place a zodiacal incense stick or cone at each of the main four compass points. If you cannot find your zodiacal incense, sandalwood or frankincense are good all-purpose incenses.

* In the centre of the circle, place your birth crystal on a cloth or small pillow.

* Light the candle in the north of the circle and then, going in a clockwise direction, each of the others, saying:

Bring light and love, power, blessing and protection, you healing angels (or name your special angel) *in this my healing work. May the circle of light remain unbroken.*

* Sit in the south, just inside the circle of candles and allow an image of a healing angel or benign power to form.

* Light next the incense, beginning again in the north, saying:

Bring your blessings too, powers of the Air, carried on this fragrant smoke, to guard and guide me as I work within this sacred circle, that I may endeavour only for the greatest goodness the better to heal and help others.

* Take the crystal and pass it clockwise once above each candle, saying:

May healing light and cleansing fire enter this crystal, cleanse, empower and magnify that the radiance may increase ever within me.

* Pass the crystal next through the fragrant smoke of each incense stick, saying:

May the purifying and restorative power of Air release the powers within this crystal to flow freely in and through me that my own healing energies and powers of renewal may likewise grow and flow freely into others and into the world.

* Take the crystal in your power hand and lightly touch first the centre of your head close to the hair line, then the centre of your brow, your heart, your navel and your womb or genitals, saying:

Mind, spirit, heart, body and fertility grow and flourish ever within me.

* If there is pain or illness in any part of your body, gently circle the crystal above it first three times anti-clockwise, then three times clockwise, saying:

Bless and heal.

* Return the crystal to the pillow and sit quietly, allowing images and words to form in your mind. Make contact perhaps with the angel of your birth crystal or with the deep unconscious wisdom collected over many millennia that we can all quite spontaneously access at such times of quiet contemplation.
* When you are ready, blow out the candles one by one, beginning with the last one you lit and continuing anti-clockwise.
* As you do so, see the light entering your crystal.
* Leave burning only the candle in the north, the first one you lit.
* Face the candle of the north and say:

The circle of light remains unbroken and lives on in my heart and mind to bless and protect even in the darkest hours of the night.

* Let the candle and incense burn through. If you wish to begin the work with your healing book, light a single white candle as well. Otherwise sit quietly, enjoying a warm drink and listening to soft music as your mind weaves crystalline images.
* Place your birth crystal under your pillow when you go to bed and keep it close to you as you dream.

Elemental signs

Each of the birth signs is ruled by an element, either Earth, Air, Fire or Water. Certain crystals have strong associations with one particular element. These elemental crystals can be powerful in healing a person whose sign belongs to that element, as they will offer an instant, natural affinity. So if, for example, you want a pink stone either for general healing or as a chakra crystal and you are born under Pisces, a Water sign, pink coral would be a good choice as it will already be tuned into your vibrations.

Some stones contain a mixture of elements, so I have listed only those where the link is strong. You can also use a stone ruled by another element if you suddenly need that elemental strength in your life.

Earth stones

These relate most strongly to people born under the Sun signs of Taurus, Virgo and Capricorn. They offer grounding, the removal of anxiety, stability, perseverance, and endurance.

They include agates, emerald, jet, leopardskin jasper, obsidian, rose quartz, rutilated quartz, smoky quartz and tiger's eye.

Earth signs can use an Air crystal to bring movement to a stagnant period, Fire crystals to burn away inertia and Water crystals to connect with other people's feelings and personal intuition.

Air stones
These are connected to Gemini, Libra and Aquarius, and offer logic, balance, adaptability and focus.

They include amethyst, clear crystal quartz, citrine, diamond, lapis lazuli, sodalite, sugilite, sapphire and turquoise.

Air signs can use Earth crystals to prevent fickleness or inability to settle to a routine but essential task; they can also work with Fire crystals to prevent ambivalence and indifference and Water crystals to soften a critical manner or contempt of those with less ability.

Fire stones
These are linked to Aries, Leo and Sagittarius. They offer energy, confidence, power and enthusiasm.

They include amber, blood agate, bloodstone, carnelian, garnet, haematite, iron pyrites, ruby, topaz and turquoise.

Fire signs can use Earth crystals to prevent burn-out, Air crystals to shape ideas and focus unrealistic expectations and Water crystals to prevent cruelty to and domination of others.

Water stones
These relate most strongly to Cancer, Scorpio and Pisces and offer intuitive awareness, sensitivity and regeneration.

They include aquamarine, calcite, coral, jade, moonstone, fluorite, pearl, opal and tourmaline.

Water signs can use Earth crystals to prevent the squandering of time and resources, Air crystals to counter over-sentimentality and conflicting aims, and Fire crystals to channel dreams into action and bring them into reality.

Using elemental crystals
Excesses of any one element can lead to imbalances at all levels of existence. It is therefore a good idea to buy one of each of the elemental crystals to counter these effects. Carry them with you, or soak them for eight hours in water, which can then be drunk to obtain the same effect.

For instant balance, place an Earth crystal in the north of a room where you sleep, relax or work. Have an Air crystal in the east, a Fire crystal in the south and a Water crystal in the west. If you wear or carry your birth crystal, your own element will naturally predominate, but you can benefit from the continuous positive qualities of the other elements as well.

Air, Earth and Fire crystals absorb energies from sunlight while Water crystals prefer moonlight.

Chapter 11
Your 50 Crystals for Healing

In this section I have drawn together the crystals referred to in different parts of the book and added others that have powerful therapeutic properties. Under each type of stone, I have listed the general properties and then added special healing qualities of the different shades.

Healing crystals do seem to have a positive effect on a variety of physical, mental and spiritual ills. Where a crystal is said to open a chakra, this means that it activates and energises a particular psychic centre and can be used for clearing blockages there. However, it is important to note that none of these stones should be used as a substitute for medical treatment in acute or serious conditions.

Agates
Category of stone: Chalcedony
Colours: Opaque, red, orange, yellow, brown, black, both banded and single colour

Agates bring emotional and physical balance and stability, security, and acceptance of oneself and others as they are. They strengthen the effects of other stones. They are especially good for stomach, colon, liver, spleen and kidneys and for blocking harmful X-rays/radiation.
Black agate: This protects against external negative forces.

Blue lace agate: Blue lace agate calms strong emotions, creating a sense of peace and encouraging patience, especially with children and in situations that cannot be changed. It cools fevers, reduces temperatures and relieves headaches. Soak in water for 12 hours and use the water as a gargle to cure sore throats. Blue lace agate also slows down hyperactivity in children.

Green agate: Like moss agate, green agate is good for gardening and also for problems with the immune system, colon, circulation, pancreas and pulse. It restores blood-sugar balance.

Moss agate: Moss agate encourages optimism, raises blood sugar, relieves anorexia and other food-related problems, and cleanses lymph nodes. It balances emotions and, like malachite, helps with toothache.

Red (blood) agate: Blood agate and red-banded agates are good for the blood, especially circulatory problems.

Yellow agate: This assists digestion and alleviates problems with the liver and spleen. It enables the user to identify and then to take what is of worth from a situation without guilt or regrets.

Amber

Category of stone: Organic gem

Colours: Clear yellow, golden brown or orange

This petrified tree resin can be up to 50 million years old and often contains fossils. Known as the honey stone, it is said to contain the power of many suns and so has the ability to absorb negativity and protect the user from harm. It will also melt away any emotional or physical rigidity.

In the Chinese tradition, the souls of tigers pass into amber when they die and so it is also a gem of courage.

Amber improves short-term memory and increases inner clarity and confidence. It is good for stomach ailments, anxiety, soothing sore throats and inner ear complaints, and aiding digestion. It strengthens the spine, lungs and nervous system. Amber offers protection from radiation, especially X-rays, the Sun, computers and industrial pollutants.

Amazonite
Category of stone: Feldspar
Colours: Opaque, light blue/turquoise

Gentle Amazonite calms the mind and soothes the nervous system, integrating different aspects of mind, body and spirit. It opens the throat, heart and solar plexus chakras, and relieves sore throats, thyroid problems and headaches. It limits self-destructive behaviour and improves self-esteem and self-confidence.

Amethyst
Category of stone: Quartz
Colours: From pale lilac and lavender to deep purple, translucent, semi-transparent and transparent

One of the best healing stones, amethyst is effective against addictions of all kinds, including those related to alcohol and food. Amethysts heal both mind and body, especially physical ailments caused by emotion. Placed on the stomach or liver, they help to soothe stomach and gall-bladder problems.

If worn when sleeping, amethyst prevents insomnia and nightmares, and when awake, reduces anger and impatience. It relieves headaches when placed on the temples or point of pain, helps eye-strain and pains, and maintains blood-sugar balance.

Aquamarine

Category of stone: Beryl
Colours: Clear light blue, blue-green to dark blue

Aquamarine soothes away stresses, encourages honest communication and increases confidence.

Medicinally, this is a purifying crystal. Placed in water overnight, the water can be drunk to cleanse the whole body and soothe any irritations in the stomach. It is also effective for toothache and neuralgia pains in the jaw and face.

Aquamarine is good for physical problems of the throat, spleen, heart, immune system, thymus, lymph nodes, mouth and ears. It helps breathing allergies and also releases anxiety, fear and restlessness. Associated with the sea and sailors, it offers safety to all who travel, especially by water. It promotes tolerance in difficult situations. Like rose quartz, aquamarine comforts those who are experiencing intense grief.

Aventurine

Category of stone: Quartz or feldspar
Colours: Translucent dark or light green quartz

Aventurine is good for all forms of physical healing. It can either be worn around the neck to gradually release healing energies or it can be placed on the area that needs healing. It heals emotional pain and fears by clearing the heart chakra. Traditionally used to reduce fevers and inflammation in joints, it lowers stress levels and is especially soothing when added to bath water.

Azurite

Category of stone: Copper carbonate
Colours: Solid deep blue, blue-purple

Azurite amplifies innate healing abilities. It activates the brow and throat chakras, helps timid people to become more assertive and decisive and encourages clear and honest communication. It also promotes psychic awareness. Physically, azurite stimulates thyroid, sinuses, spleen and nervous system and assists with skin cleansing. Azurite reduces depression and anger.

Beryl

Category of stone: Beryl
Colours: Transparent, golden brown

Beryl stimulates the mind and nervous system and strengthens the spine and bones. A crystal of the Sun, it activates the solar plexus, throat and brow chakras and increases inner clarity and confidence. A protective crystal, beryl is good for the stomach (particularly stomach ulcers), intestines and cardio-vascular system and for counteracting nausea, exhaustion, depression, fear, resentment and eating disorders. Beryl is an anti-toxin, especially for the liver and skin.

Pink beryl: This opens the heart chakra and is also good for the heart itself. It provides stability and eases times of change. Pink beryl is protective against nightmares and children's anxieties.

Bloodstone (heliotrope)

Category of stone: Chalcedony
Colours: Opaque, mottled green and red

Bloodstone is used in modern practice to stop nosebleeds and cuts, help with menstrual cramps, improve circulation, enable easier childbirth and enhance fertility. It cleanses the heart, blood, marrow, thymus and lungs.

Boji stones
Category of stone: Iron-magnetite
Colours: Solid round, grey-brown discs with high iron content
Boji stones are powerful healers and balance body's energy field. Holding a boji stone in each hand reduces pain of all kinds and restores harmony to body, mind and spirit. Boji stones also prevent negativity from building up, create a sense of well-being and are deeply protective against all harm. They should be handled every day and exposed to light to prevent them crumbling.

Calcite
Category of stone: Feldspar
Colours: Transparent or semi-transparent milky yellow, peach, green, white or clear crystals
These are stones of integration and balance in both body and mind and gradually release energies if carried or kept in a workspace.
Blue calcite: This eases pain, especially in the back.
Green calcite: This induces tranquillity and encourages learning from experience. It helps to replace fears and destructive habits with positivity. Green calcite clears toxins from the body.
Orange calcite: An uplifting crystal, it is also helpful for kidneys and bladder.
Yellow calcite: This helps the spine and bones and assists detoxification of kidneys, pancreas and spleen, and decalcification of

joints and bones.

White calcite: White calcite encourages clearer physical vision, helps near-sightedness and promotes good health in the whole body. It is a general cleanser.

Carnelian

Category of stone: Chalcedony

Colours: Yellow, orange and red, occasionally brown, translucent

Carnelian is a crystal of courage, confidence and self-esteem. It enhances creativity, brings fertility and abundance to all aspects of life and keeps away envy and spite in others. Carnelian warms and cleanses the blood and kidneys, stimulates appetite, sexuality and physical energy, and helps the reproductive system. It relieves lower back problems, menstrual cramps, arthritis, and problems of the kidneys, gall-bladder and pancreas. Carnelian is good with food-related problems, especially where a question of identity and self-esteem is involved.

Chrysoprase

Category of stone: Chalcedony

Colours: Translucent, bright green

Known as the apple stone because of its colour, chrysoprase opens the heart chakra and makes possible flexibility and adaptability in the face of difficulties, alleviating depression, self-doubts and extreme emotional swings. It is a good stone to wear near the heart or on a cord around the neck to encourage meditation.

Citrine

Category of stone: Quartz
Colours: Clear sparkling yellow

Citrine clears energy blockages in the body. It encourages mental and emotional clarity and improves long- and short-term memory, bringing optimism and self-confidence. Citrine reduces anxiety and depression, and relieves digestive problems, stomach tension and disorders of the spleen, gall-bladder, liver, bladder and bowel. It is helpful in food allergies and food-related illnesses. It opens the solar plexus chakra and can be used to detoxify all the chakras.

Coral

Category of stone: Organic
Colours: Opaque, red and orange

Coral has been a children's stone from the time of the Ancient Greeks, when Plato wrote that it should be hung around children's necks to prevent them falling, cure colic and relieve teething pains.

Coral increases fertility, energises the body and mind, promotes healthy muscles, spine, blood and heart, and encourages bone and tissue regeneration and reproductive system, thyroid and metabolic functioning.

Pink coral: This opens the heart chakra, increasing empathy, sensitivity and compassion towards oneself and others.

White coral: An all-purpose healer of the body and of tension pains, white coral is also good for sinus problems.

Black coral: This protects against self-destructive tendencies.

Desert rose

Category of stone: Gypsum
Colours: Light brown, rough textured, opaque with glints

Desert rose looks like a wrinkled nut but has silver glints all over it, revealing the potential within. It focuses thoughts, reduces anxiety and thus reduces stress and hyperactivity.

Diamond

Category of stone: Carbon (diamond is the hardest known mineral)
Colours: Transparent sparkling white, also yellow, brown, orange, pink, lavender, blue, green and occasionally black

In legend the first diamond was discovered by Alexander the Great in about 350 BC. According to legend, the diamonds were in a valley guarded by snakes, but Alexander's men polished their shields so that when the snakes saw their own reflections they turned on themselves. Certainly diamonds have always been prized and have invoked greed and tyranny in people desperate to possess them. Despite this, when used or given in love, they are powerful healing stones. In the Middle Ages they were worn to prevent plague.

Mainly because of their brilliance, diamonds are used to clear the mind. By opening the crown chakra they can increase contact with other dimensions.

A diamond removes physical and emotional blockages and negativity and draws toxicity from the body. Use a diamond as an energiser when exhaustion or doubts set in.

Emerald

Category of stone: Beryl
Colours: Green, sparkling, transparent, sometimes cloudy

The Romans believed that emeralds were a warning stone and lost their colour or even crumbled when evil was near.

Emerald is the most powerful gemstone used in physical healing and even very small stones can be used effectively. Place the emerald on the area that needs healing or wear it around the neck for continuous healing and protective power. A stone of love, emerald open the heart chakra, relieves depression and stress-related conditions, heals sores and ulcers, helps insomnia and encourages peaceful dreams. Emeralds are good for the lungs, heart, lymph nodes, blood, thymus and pancreas, for balancing blood-sugar levels and for easing childbirth. Emerald also relieves eye problems, and water in which an emerald has been soaked is traditionally used to bathe sore eyes. It assists relaxation and meditation and strengthens clairvoyant and psychic abilities.

Fluorite

Category of stone: Fluorite halide/flurospar
Colours: Rainbow shades

A gentle yet powerful healer in all its forms, fluorite harmonises body, mind and spirit and promotes physical and emotional clarity. It is good for spleen, bones, arthritic conditions, teeth and lungs, for healing scars and for reducing toxicity, anxiety, and insomnia.

Blue fluorite: This is good for throat, nose and ears and encourages self-forgiveness.

Clear and purple fluorite: These clear stagnation in body and mind and are good for cleansing the aura. They open the brow chakra and so increase psychic awareness. Both colours are helpful for eyesight, sinuses and warding off colds; their power amplifies that of other crystals.

Green fluorite: This opens the heart chakra, stills the mind and heart, and harmonises and energises all the chakras. This stone is helpful for hormonal changes such as PMS and menopause.

Lavender fluorite: This brings a sense of inner peace, serenity and harmony with nature and the life force. In clusters, it lowers both domestic and work-related stress and can be placed either in the workplace or home to absorb negativity and hyperactivity.

Garnet

Category of stone: Silicate
Colours: Shining dark red, dark red, green, orange and colourless

Shining garnet is best for healing. A protective stone, it was used by Eastern European peoples against illness, night phantoms and all forms of manifest evil, including the mythical vampire. It is very protective for travellers, especially against attack.

Garnets are natural energisers both of mind and body. They open the root and sacral chakras. They are warming and so helpful for relieving arthritis, painful or strained muscles and stiff limbs, and for strengthening blood and the heart and improving circulation. A stone of fertility, garnet stimulates sexuality and balances hormones; it is also good for kidney problems and gallstones.

Hawk's eye (falcon's eye)
Category of stone: Quartz
Colours: Green, grey or blue

Hawk's eye is good for improving mental and physical vision and concentration. It opens the solar plexus and brow chakras, bringing spirituality into the sphere of action. It is a protective crystal that endows courage.

Haematite
Category of stone: Related to iron ore
Colours: Silver-grey metallic brilliance

Haematite is a powerful earthing and protective stone that activates the root chakra, focuses indecision, aids concentration, improves memory and helps all forms of study. It builds confidence and self-esteem, and strengthens determination and courage. Strongly linked to physical health, it is good for spleen and blood. It also acts as a shield against physical and emotional hostility and is effective for overcoming jet lag and for easing childbirth.

Jade

Category of stone: Jadite and nephrite, silicates
Colours: Shades of green, opaque to translucent

A stone for health, prosperity and long life, in the Orient, jade was associated with reincarnation. Jade bowls were used for food to energise it with the life force.

The Romans called jade *lapis nephriticus,* 'the kidney stone', because of the belief it could cure kidney problems.

Jade, like rose quartz and coral, is a stone for children because of its gentleness. It offers wisdom, quiet courage, emotional balance, peace and inner harmony. It is good for the lungs, heart, thymus, immune system, kidneys, arthritis (especially in hip joints), and for relieving fluid retention. It promotes male fertility and blood detoxification and is a tonic for the whole nervous system.

Jasper

Category of stone: Quartz
Colours: Opaque, multi-coloured, also single colours of yellow, orange, brown and green; sometimes found as petrified wood

Jasper was worn as an amulet over the stomach to aid digestion and to prevent internal bleeding.

Black jasper: Protects against all negative influences and especially the user's own repressed feelings. It is good for absorbing anger.

Brown jasper: Sharpens the five senses and gives stability in times of upheaval.

Green jasper: Opens the heart chakra; good for all healing, especially general tissue regeneration, for the lungs and for the absorption of minerals from food and herbs. It soothes bad dreams, strengthens bones and eases childbirth.

Leopardskin jasper: Helps a person to make positive changes without regrets or guilt.

Red jasper: A defence against hostility; helps fevers and blood disorders.

Yellow jasper: Good for the digestion, stomach, intestines, liver and spleen areas; counters the effects of jealousy, spite and unfair criticism.

Jet

Category of stone: Organic
Colour: Black

Jet is fossilised wood. Amulets of this mineral have been found in very ancient graves. It guards against bad dreams and relieves toothache, neuralgia, female reproductive problems and all pains or swellings in the lower body, legs and feet; psychologically, it helps users to resolve grief.

Kunzite

Category of stone: Spodumene
Colours: Pink, lilac, transparent

This is sometimes known as the woman's stone, because of its ability to heal all female disorders. Good for overcoming compulsive behaviour and addictions, it restores confidence and reduces depression, extreme mood swings and stress. If kept in the car, kunzite will reduce road rage and tensions caused by commuting, as well as stress at work.

Labradorite
Category of stone: Feldspar
Colours: Subtle green, blue, yellow, metallic, iridescent

Labradorite promotes restful sleep and helps the user to retain empathy with other people without sacrificing identity or personal priorities. It unblocks any chakra.

Lapis lazuli
Category of stone: Lazurite
Colours: Opaque, rich, medium to dark blue with flecks of iron pyrites (fool's gold)

Known as the eye of wisdom, lapis lazuli can open the brow chakra, increasing intuitive abilities, clairvoyance and connection to the higher self, as well as increasing idealism and altruism. Lapis also opens the throat chakra, encouraging honest but wise communication. It counteracts insomnia and shyness and helps with inflammation and pain, especially headaches and eye strain. Lapis is deeply protective.

Malachite

Category of stone: Copper carbonate
Colours: Green with black stripes

A purifier and energiser, malachite replaces negativity with positive energies and pain with warmth. It opens the brow chakra for psychic vision and also improves physical sight and concentration. It is excellent for teeth and gums, especially for relieving toothache if held above the painful tooth. It promotes tissue regeneration and is good for the stomach, liver, kidneys and lungs, and for boosting the immune system and circulation.

Malachite draws out pain, inflammation, depression and anger, cleanses the auric field and is excellent for counteracting technological pollution. However, malachite should not be used by children or pets as it can be poisonous.

Moonstone (selenite)

Category of stone: Feldspar
Colours: Translucent with white, fawn pink, yellow, occasionally blue sheen

A stone of gardening and fertility, both of plants and of women, moonstone offers a path to inner wisdom, increased intuition and clairvoyance. It heals hormonal problems in both sexes, troubles with fluid retention, PMT, menstrual and fertility problems and menopausal disorders, especially hot flushes. Moonstones also relieve anxiety and nightmares, especially in children.

Mother of pearl
Category of stone: Organic
Colours: Iridescent white/pink

This is not a stone as such but the lining of oyster shells. It is, however, formed into oval stones and beads. It carries the peaceful healing energy of the sea and soothes extremes of emotions, protecting against over-sensitivity and stress. It is good for new-born babies and eases their first few months of life.

Obsidian (Apache tears)
Category of stone: Lava (magma)
Colour: Translucent, black and white

Linked to the root chakra, obsidian brings light and eases grief, sorrow and guilt, encouraging optimism for the future. It protects sensitive people from negativity.
Snowflake obsidian: Assists clairaudience and begins the process of learning to trust and love again.

Onyx
Category of stone: Chalcedony
Colours: Black, blue, green and yellow

Onyx calms intense mood swings and emotions. It is good for concentrated healing but needs frequent cleansing and recharging.
Black onyx: This opens the root chakra and helps to change bad habits. Good for chakra work.
Green onyx: This opens the heart chakra and balances emotions.

Opal

Category of stone: Silica

Colours: Iridescent white, cream, fire (rainbow) and black

The Greeks called the opal *opthalmios* or 'eye-stone', because it was said to improve weak eye-sight and was an aid to seeing into the future as well as past scenes. It opens the crown and brow chakras and so increases intuitive thinking, significant dreams and healing. Opals are beneficial for glandular problems and for fluid retention.

Black opal: Strengthens the bones.

Fire opal: Helpful for sexual problems, especially in women.

White opal: This can ease childbirth, enhance natural beauty and improve respiration, especially asthma attacks or bronchitis.

Pearl

Category of stone: Organic

Colours: Iridescent, pale cream or white, black, grey, pink and blue

Pearls can reflect a wearer's ill-health and may grow paler or dull if the person is unwell.

They can protect against anger and stress and increase self-esteem. They open the solar plexus chakra and so aid digestion. They heal stomach and gall-bladder ailments and boost the immune system. Pearls heal best without other gems. Cleanse them frequently.

Black pearls: These attract prosperity and abundance of all kinds.

Pink pearl: A stone of the heart, pink pearl brings love and affection; a good stone for children.

White pearl: Symbol of pure heart and mind, this stone encourages faith in self and others.

Peridot

Category of stone: Gem form of olivine, a magnesium iron silicate
Colours: Clear, transparent bright green, green-yellow

Good for alleviating jealousy, depression, anger, fear and anxiety, peridot can encourage mental clarity, patience and a positive attitude. Peridot clears the heart chakra and strengthens the innate life force. The yellow shades of peridot also open the solar plexus chakra and so help stomach, liver and adrenal conditions. Peridot stimulates tissue regeneration.

Pyrite (fool's gold)

Category of stone: Iron sulphide
Colour: Dark, rock-like with gold inclusions; can be polished to form a rich golden translucent crystal

This stone can provide focus, improve logic and memory, clear confused thoughts and indecision, and ease anxiety, frustration and depression. It strengthens the solar plexus chakra, healing stomach, gall-bladder and intestinal troubles and ulcers. Pyrites help the effective use of minerals by the body.

Quartz

Category of stone: Crystal

Colours: Transparent or semi-transparent in a variety of colours, also cloudy or opaque

Clear or white quartz: Clear crystal quartz opens both the brow and crown chakras. Use a round crystal directly on a headache. Rubbed on gums it can relieve toothache or, held in the hand, reduce a temperature. Clear crystal spheres were traditionally used to concentrate the rays of the Sun upon a diseased or painful area of the body or in the direction of a malfunctioning internal organ.

Blue quartz (also grey and lavender): Clears the throat chakra and strengthens the connection with the brow chakra. It can ease throat pain and tension, and stimulates effective functioning of the immune system.

Frosted/snow/milky quartz: Worn by nursing mothers to promote lactation and to help babies to digest milk.

Rose quartz: Known as the children's stone because it is so gentle, this eases pain or tension and speeds healing of cuts or bruises. It promotes family love and friendship, brings peace and forgiveness and helps mend quarrels. It soothes and warms the heart, physically and emotionally, keeps away nightmares and night fears and protects against cold.

Rutilated quartz: This is a clear quartz with metallic, golden rutile, copper, or blue/grey titanium fibres. It is said to heal all inner ills, emotional and physical. It amplifies healing energy and thoughts, opening the crown and brow chakras. It can increase natural immunity, stamina and physical and mental strength, and is good for tissue regeneration, boosting the immune system and easing depression.

Smoky quartz: This is traditionally associated with removing negative influences. It encourages the assimilation of protein by the body and is also good for increasing fertility and relieving all forms of reproductive disorders (especially in women), PMS and menstrual and menopausal difficulties. It alleviates anxiety, depression and repeated destructive emotional patterns, and encourages relaxation.

Rhodocrosite
Category of stone: Manganese
Colours: Opaque to clear pink

Rhodocrosite has more intense energies than rose quartz and can unblock the heart and solar plexus chakras. It is good for overcoming stress-related stomach problems, food addictions, anorexia, bulimia, food cravings, asthma and other allergies and problems with the eyes.

Rhodonite
Category of stone: Silicate and manganese
Colour: Opaque pink with black inclusions

Stimulates the heart chakra and prevents nightmares, calming stress and anger. Traditionally a remedy for speech and hearing problems and for chest diseases such as emphysema and asthma.

Ruby

Category of stone: Corundum, the second hardest known mineral
Colour: Sparkling red

This can open the heart chakra, strengthening the physical and emotional heart. Ruby restores energy after exhaustion and is effective against cuts and bruises, infections of the reproductive system and menstrual problems, psychological or stress-related sexual dysfunction and high cholesterol. It boosts healthy circulation, regulates the menstrual flow and ensures effective blood-sugar functioning.

Sapphire

Category of stone: Corundum
Colours: Sparkling blue, green, pink, purple, clear

Related to ruby, sapphire brings mental clarity, clearing confusion and redundant guilt and resentments.
Blue sapphire: Linked with the throat chakra, this stone enhances clear communication. An anti-depressant, it is good for the nervous system, memory, and pituitary and thyroid glands. It reduces inflammation and high temperatures, and relieves burns and hearing and sinus difficulties. It is most potent if directly in contact with the skin.
Star sapphire: More subtle in its effects, it reduces anxiety levels and indecision and shields against pollutants.

Sodalite

Category of stone: Feldspathoid
Colours: Deep blue, sometimes flecked with white, indigo

Sodalite enhances clear, honest communication and promotes logical thinking, but also creativity, idealism and altruism. It alleviates subconscious guilt and fears. It balances body energy levels, promotes healthy functioning of the lymphatic system and is good for the throat, neck, mouth and ears and for blood-sugar levels. Sodalite relieves insomnia, burns, sinus infections and high blood pressure.

Spinel

Category of stone: Magnesium aluminate
Colours: Transparent, colourless (pure form), black, blue, green, purple, pink

Spinel alleviates stress and depression and is a mental and physical energiser, especially in its colourless form. It detoxifies the body and is good with other forms of healing, for example herbs.
Red spinel: This renews strength and stamina and triggers survival instincts in times of crisis. Traditionally it is especially favourable to health professionals and healers.

Sugilite

Category of stone: Luvulite (royal azele), sodium, potassium and iron minerals
Colour: Opaque rich purple

A relatively expensive stone but valuable for healing – good for removing headaches, inflammation, toxins and emotional blocks and for reducing stress levels. Placed on the forehead, it alleviates depression. It brings balance to the major glands of the body.

Sunstone

Category of stone: Aventurine feldspar
Colours: Translucent, reddish, gold-orange with a metallic sheen
A restorer of life and hope to mind, body and spirit. Good for the blood, heart and circulation and for warming aching bones or joints.

Tiger's eye

Category of stone: Chalcedony
Colours: Yellow-gold and brown stripes, burgundy stripes

Also known as cat's eye, tiger's eye is associated with the practical aspects of life and enhances health in the five senses. It is a stone of balance, reducing desire for excesses of food or alcohol; emotionally it offers a sense of perspective and the ability to see other people's points of view.

Tiger's eye strengthens the solar plexus chakra and helps digestive processes, stomach and gall-bladder problems and ulcers. It heals bruises, warms aching bones and is helpful for beginning detoxification.

Topaz

Category of stone: Aluminum silicate
Colours: Clear golden, champagne-coloured, pink, pale blue, orange or brown

Topaz guards against nightmares and night terrors as well as violent emotion. Water in which a topaz has been soaked relieves insomnia if drunk an hour before bedtime. It is also helpful for alleviating women's ailments, disorders of the stomach and problems with the throat, nose, mouth and lungs.

Golden topaz: This controls anxiety conditions, severe mood swings, insomnia, worries, physical exhaustion, mental distress and nervous stomach disorders. Good for detoxifying the liver and pancreas, regenerating tissue and bones, and balancing blood sugar.

Tourmaline
Category of stone: Borosilicate
Colours: Black, blue, green, pink, watermelon (green, pink and red striped)

Tourmaline strengthens body and spirit. Clearer stones are especially effective for the nervous system and for detoxifying the blood and lymph glands. Tourmaline in all shades dispels fear, negativity and sorrows, encourages peaceful sleep and eases compulsions.

Black tourmaline: This protects against hostile feelings and negative intentions in others. It relieves arthritis, adrenal gland troubles and constipation.

Blue tourmaline (indicolite): Linked with the throat chakra, it rejuvenates and harmonises the nervous system and is good for the lungs.

Green tourmaline: Balances emotions so that they do not drain physical energies. It restores enthusiasm and optimism and encourages abundance in all spheres of life, soothes the central nervous system, triggers the immune system and offers healing for neuralgia, migraine, burns, asthma and other stress-related allergies as well as ailments of the female reproductive system.

Pink tourmaline: This heals emotional and physical pain and gives comfort and relief in chronic or severe illness. It enhances fertility and creativity in both the physical and mental spheres.

Watermelon tourmaline: This is especially potent in cases of severe illness, triggering the immune system and endocrinal glands; it amplifies the effects of other tourmalines in healing. It is good for the heart.

Turquoise
Category of stone: Phosphate of aluminium with copper and traces of iron
Colours: Opaque, light blue or blue-green

Turquoise has been regarded as a healer for all sicknesses in many cultures and ages. It opens the throat chakra, encouraging honest communication from the heart, creativity, serenity and spirituality. It detoxifies the system of alcohol, pollution, X-rays and solar radiation and alleviates anorexia and food-related disorders, migraines and anxiety. It is effective against sore throats, rheumatism, arthritis and bone disorders, as well as inner ear and eye problems, lung and chest infections, asthma and other allergies, tooth and gum disorders and high blood pressure.

Useful Contacts

Crystals, incenses, magical supplies
Australia
Future Pastimes
24a Collins Street
Kiama
New South Wales

The Mystic Trader
125 Flinders Lane
Melbourne 3000

Mysterys
Level 1
314–22 Darling Street
Balmain
New South Wales

South Africa
The Wellstead
1 Wellington Avenue
Wynberg
Cape 7300

UK
Futhark
18 Halifax Road
Todmorden
Lancs
OL14 5AD

Mandragora
Essex House
Thame
OX9 3LS

Mysteries
7 Monmouth Street
London
WC2H 9DA

Pentagram
11 Cheapside
Wakefield
WF1 2SD

US
Eye of the Cat
3314 East Broadway
Long Beach
CA 90803

The Crystal Cave
415 West Foothill Boulevard
Claremont
CA 91711

Open Door Metaphysical
Shoppe
428 North Buchanan Circle
Suite 16
Pacheco
California 94553

Spirit Search Emporium
Sun Angel Innovations
3939 West Windmills Boulevard
2060 Chandler
Arizona 85226

Candles
Australia
Price's Candles Pty Ltd
18 Gibson Avenue
Padstow
NSW 2211

UK
Price's Patent Candle Company
10 York Road
London
SW11 3RU

US
Wax Wonders
221 North Main Street
Versailles
Kentucky 40383

Herbs
UK
Gerard House
736 Christchurch Road
Bournemouth
Dorset
BH7 6BZ

US
Planet Herbs
815 2nd Avenue
Marlinton
WV 24954

Incenses
US
Tibetan Incense Company
53 South 200 East Kanab
Utah 84741

Meditation/Visualisation/
Shamanic Music
Australia
New World Productions
PO Box 244 WBO
Red Hill
Queensland 4059

UK
Stress Busters
Beechwood Music
Littleton House
11 Littleton Road
Ashford
TW15 1UU

US
Raven Recordings
744 Broad Street
Room 1815
Newark
New Jersey 07102

Smudging equipment
(smudge sticks, herbs,
incenses, etc.)
Australia
Eartharomas Earthcraft
Magpie Flats Herb Farm
273–95 Boyle Road
Kenilworth
Qld 4574

UK
Dreamcatcher Trading
47 Bruce Road
Sheffield
South Yorkshire
S11 8QD

US
Arizona Gateway Trading Post
Mail-HC 37
Box 919-UPS 14265
North Hiway 93
Golden Valley
AZ 86413

Spiritual healing

Australia
Australian Spiritualist
Association
PO Box 248
Canterbury
New South Wales 2193

Canada
National Federation of Spiritual
Healers (Canada)
Toronto
Ontario

UK
British Alliance of Healing
Associations
Mrs Jo Wallace
3 Sandy Lane
Gisleham
Lowestoft
Suffolk
NR 33 8EQ

National Federation of Spiritual
Healers
Old Manor Farm Studio
Church Street
Sunbury on Thames
Middlesex
TW16 6RG

US
World of Light
PO Box 425
Wappingers Falls
NY 12590
(Can provide list of healers)

Cassandra's website is
www.Cassandraeason.co.uk

Further Reading

Crystals and crystal healing

Bravo, Brett, *Crystal Healing Secrets,* Warner Books Inc., New York, 1988

Bourgault, Luc, *The American Indian Secrets of Crystal Healing,* Quantum, 1997

Campbell, Dan, *Edgar Cayce on the Power of Color, Stones and Crystals,* Warner Books Inc., 1989

Cunningham, Scott, *The Encyclopaedia of Crystal, Gem and Metal Magic,* Llewellyn, St Paul, Minnesota, 1991

Eason, Cassandra, *Crystals Talk to the Woman Within,* Quantum, 2000

Galde, Phyllis, *Crystal Healing, The Next Step,* Llewellyn Books, St Paul, Minnesota, 1991

Silbey, Uma, *The Complete Crystal Guidebook,* Bantam Books, New York, 1986

Williams, Cornelio Maries, *Gemstones and Color,* The Triad Publising Co., West Hartford, Connecticut, 1985

Auras and chakras

Andrews, Ted, *How to See and Read the Aura,* Llewellyn, St Paul, Minnesota, 1994

Arewa, Shola Caroline, *Opening to Spirit,* Thorsons, 1999

Brennan, Barbara Ann, *Hands of Light, A Guide to Healing Through the Human Energy Field,* Bantam Books, New York, 1987

Eason, Cassandra, *Aura Reading,* Piatkus Books, 2000

Astrology
Fenton, Sasha, *Predicting the Future,* Piatkus Books, 1999
Gettings, Fred, *Arkana Dictionary of Astrology,* Arkana, 1990

Candles
Bruce, Marie, *Candleburning Rituals,* Foulsham, 2001
Buckland, Ray, *Advanced Candle Magick,* Llewellyn, St Paul, Minnesota, 1997
Buckland, Ray, *Practical Candleburning Rituals,* Llewellyn, St Paul, Minnesota, 1982
Eason, Cassandra, *Candle Power,* Blandford, 1999

Herbs and incenses
Culpeper, N., *Culpeper's Colour Herbal,* Foulsham, 1983
Cunningham, Scott, *The Complete Book of Oils, Incenses and Brews,* Llewellyn, St Paul, Minnesota, 1991
Cunningham, Scott, *The Encyclopaedia of Magical Herbs,* Llewellyn, St Paul, Minnesota, 1987

Smudging and Native American spirituality
Alexander, Jane, *The Smudging and Blessings Pack,* Sterling, New York, 1998
Eason, Cassandra, *Smudging and Incense Burning,* Quantum, 2001
Wakpski, Diane, *Smudging,* Black Sparrow Press, US, 1996

Index